I0113486

The Shopping Addiction Workbook

Information, Assessments, and Tools for Managing Life with a Behavioral Addiction

Ester R.A. Leutenberg and John J. Liptak, EdD

Whole Person Associates
Mental Health & Wellness Publishers
Duluth, Minnesota

Whole Person Associates

101 West 2nd Street, Suite 203
Duluth, MN 55802-5004

800-247-6789

Books@WholePerson.com
WholePerson.com

The Shopping Addiction Workbook

Printed in the United States of America

Editorial Director: Jack Kosmach
Art Director: Mathew Pawlak
Cover Design: Adam Sippola
Editor: Peg Johnson

Library of Congress Control Number: 2022942261
ISBN:978-1-57025-368-3

From the co-authors, Ester and John,
Our gratitude, thanks, and appreciation
to the following professionals:

❧ ○ ❧

Editorial Directors – Jack Kosmach and Peg Johnson

Editor and Lifelong Teacher – Eileen Regen, MEd, CIE

Reviewers – Niki Tilicki, MA Ed • Eileen Jonatis, MA Ed

Proofreader – Jay Leutenberg, CASA

Art Director – Mathew Pawlak

❧ ○ ❧

A Special Thank You
to
Whole Person Associates

for their interest in mental health issues.

Free PDF Download Available
To access your free PDF download of the assessment tools
and all of the reproducible activities in this workbook, go to:
https://WholePerson.com/store/TheShoppingAddictionWorkbook2261.html

Understanding Behavioral Addictions

Many types of addictions exist. Behavioral addictions that have been talked about most have been substance abuse addictions. However, a behavioral addiction can develop and take the same form as a physical dependence on a substance.

> ...it is the compulsive nature of the behavior that is often indicative of an individual's behavioral or process addiction. The compulsion to continually engage in an activity or behavior despite the negative impact on the person's ability to remain mentally or physically healthy and functional in the home and community defines behavioral addiction. The person may find the behavior rewarding psychologically or get a "high" while engaged in the activity but may later feel guilt, remorse, or even overwhelmed by the consequences of that continued choice. Unfortunately, as is typical for all who struggle with addiction, people living with behavioral addictions are unable to stop engaging in the behavior for any length of time without treatment and intervention.
>
> People are increasingly experiencing non-substance behavioral addictions and diminished control over the behavior. No longer categorized as impulse disorders, behavioral addictions are now viewed as true addictions like substance abuse.

~ American Addiction Centers (2019)

The National Institute of Health (2010) states the following:

> Growing evidence suggests that behavioral addictions resemble substance addictions in many domains, including natural history, phenomenology, tolerance, comorbidity, overlapping genetic contribution, neurobiological mechanisms, and response to treatment.

The concept of addiction, for many years adopted solely to indicate the use of psychotropic substances, is now being applied to describe a heterogeneous group of syndromes known as "behavioral addictions," "no-drug addictions," or "new addictions." Prevalence rates for such conditions, taken as a whole, are among the highest for mental disorders with social, cultural, and economic implications. Individual forms of behavioral addictions are linked by a series of psychopathological features that include repetitive, persistent, and dysfunctional behaviors; loss of control over behavior despite the negative repercussions of the latter; compulsion to satisfy the need to implement the behavior; initial well-being produced by the behavior; craving; onset of tolerance; abstinence; and, ultimately, a progressive, significant impairment of overall individual functioning.

Why Are They Called Behavioral Addictions?

Behavioral addictions constitute any maladaptive pattern of excessive behavior that manifests in physiological, psychological, and cognitive symptoms such as the following:

- **Continuance:** individual continues the behavior despite knowing that this activity is creating or exacerbating physical, psychological, or interpersonal problems.

- **Intention effects:** individual is unable to stick to routines as evidenced by exceeding the amount of time devoted to the behavior or consistently going beyond the intended amount.

- **Lack of control:** unsuccessful attempts to reduce the level of the behavior or cease it for a certain period of time.

- **Reduction in activities:** as a direct result of the behavior, the person reduces or stops social, familial, occupational, or recreational activities.

- **Time:** much time is spent preparing for, engaging in, and recovering from the behavior.

- **Tolerance:** individual increases the amount of the behavior to feel the desired effect, be it a "buzz" or a sense of accomplishment.

- **Withdrawal:** in the absence of the behavior, the person experiences negative effects such as anxiety, irritability, restlessness, and sleep problems.

Addiction to Shopping

It was not until the 1990s that researchers presented evidence that shopping addiction was widespread. Most definitions of shopping addictions agree that this psychiatric condition is characterized by excessive or poorly controlled urges or behaviors related to shopping and spending, which inadvertently lead to negative consequences *(e.g., marked subjective distress, interference in social or occupational functioning, and financial/legal problems).*

In general, shopping and spending tendencies:
- Are strongly related to social attitudes toward money, personal finances, and materialistic values.
- Exist as separate conditions that may not necessarily be correlated with negative emotions.
- May not necessarily be pathological and should first be seen as representing an extreme form of shopping behavior before being diagnosed as an addiction.

Shopping addiction is characterized by excessive shopping cognitions and buying behaviors that lead to distress or impairment. The disorder occurs mainly in women, has an onset in the late teen years or early 20s, and appears to be chronic or recurrent. People experiencing a shopping addiction are preoccupied with shopping, experience pre-purchase tension or anxiety, and a sense of relief following a purchase.

Shopping addiction is associated with mood and anxiety disorders, substance use disorders, eating disorders, and personality disorders. Shopping addiction disorder tends to run in families with mood and substance use disorders.

SHOPPING ADDICTION IN THE DSM-5

Although absent from the present diagnostic guidelines such as the World Health Organizations (2018) International Classification of Diseases (ICD) and the American Psychiatric Association's (2018) Diagnostic and Statistical Manual of Mental Disorders (DSM-5), experts have recognized that shopping behavior can quickly and easily become an addiction and lead to physical, occupational, social, and psychological problems. Shopping addiction is expected to be included in the next updated version of the DSM.

Marcelo Piquet-Pessôa, Gabriela M. Ferreira, Isabela A. Melca and Leonardo F. Fontenelle (2014) suggested that although many behavioral addictions are being included in the DSM-5, there is still debate on whether other less recognized forms of impulsive behaviors, such as compulsive shopping and buying can be conceptualized as addictions. Some of the reasons for this determination include:
1) The diagnosis requires evidence of severe distress or a major interference in a person's social, financial, and occupational functioning.
2) There must be a distinction between compulsive buyers, normal consumers, and hoarders with excessive acquisition as the focus and excitement not on the item bought, but on the buying process itself.
3) In compulsive shopping, the overpowering urge to buy, the repetitive loss of control overspending, and the negative emotional state typically emerges when the person is not buying resemble craving, drug seeking behavior, and withdrawal symptoms in substance use disorders.

People addicted to shopping tend to show high impulsivity, low self-esteem, vulnerability to negative emotions, and susceptibility to cultural influence. Shopping behavior is experienced as a relief from negative emotions. After purchasing unnecessary or overly expensive items, when checks bounce or credit card limits are breached, people tend to feel guilty. They hide their expenses from family members and friends, but when the unpleasant sensation returns, they buy again.

The constant preoccupation with shopping and spending can be a behavioral addiction that can be effectively treated using a range of cognitive and behavioral therapies.

Potential Signs of Shopping Addiction

One can have a shopping addiction without being totally out of control. An addiction to shopping is evident when shopping behaviors disrupt various aspects of one's life, including intimate relationships, family, friendships, and workplace performance. As the intensity of one's shopping behavior increases, the person is at risk of becoming addicted to shopping.

Like most people addicted to something, those addicted to shopping usually try to hide their addiction from everyone, including their loved one(s). If they lie about their purchases or hide credit card bills, purchased items, shopping bags, and receipts from purchases, they are at risk of becoming or are already addicted to shopping. An addiction to shopping can be seen in people who shop online, those who shop in person, and those who use a combination of shopping formats.

Symptoms of a Person with a Shopping Disorder

- Maxes out credit cards.
- Cannot pay off debts.
- Feels a high when shopping.
- Lies to continue shopping.
- Spends money that is not available.
- Does anything to get a good bargain.
- Thinks about going shopping all the time.
- Demonstrates poor money management skills.
- Feels euphoric rushes during and after shopping.
- Uses shopping to cope with stress.
- Shows an inability to control shopping behavior.
- Undergoes problems in life due to over shopping.
- Goes shopping as a reaction to feeling angry or sad.
- Worries about money because of shopping behavior.
- Buys unnecessary items or items that never get used.
- Has conflicts with loved ones about their need to shop.
- Experiences problems at work due to shopping behavior.

- Steals money from others, including loved ones, to shop.
- Suffers guilt or embarrassment after a shopping spree.
- Intends to buy a few items and ends up buying much more.
- Accumulates debt and dire financial straits due to overspending.
- Obsesses over making purchases on a daily or weekly basis.
- Fails when attempting to stop compulsive shopping behavior.
- Hides purchased items from family and friends because of guilt.
- Shops to feel less guilty about previous shopping sprees.
- Endures regret or remorse about purchases and continues to shop.
- Awareness of intense euphoria or excitement after purchasing items.
- Opens new credit card accounts without paying off balances on other cards.
- Experiences overwhelming urges to buy things, that must be gratified instantly.
- Damages personal relationships because of lying, shopping, and overspending.

Those with a mild shopping addiction may exhibit between 4 and 5 of these behaviors. In contrast, those with a moderately severe shopping addiction may show 6 to 7 behaviors. People who suffer from a severe shopping addiction exhibits most of the behaviors.

Types of Shopping Disorders

According to Shulman (2008), one can identify several different types of shopping addictions:

1. Compulsive shopaholics who shop when they are feeling emotional distress.
2. Trophy shopaholics who are always shopping for the perfect item.
3. Shopaholics who want the image of being a big spender and owner of flashy items.
4. Bargain seekers who purchase items they don't need because the items are on sale.
5. Shoppers who get caught in a vicious cycle of buying and returning.
6. Collectors who don't feel complete unless they have one item in each color or every piece of a set.
7. Online shoppers who can use technology to order any time of the day, all year.

Relationship Addiction

An addiction to shopping is much like any other addiction. The process looks something like this:

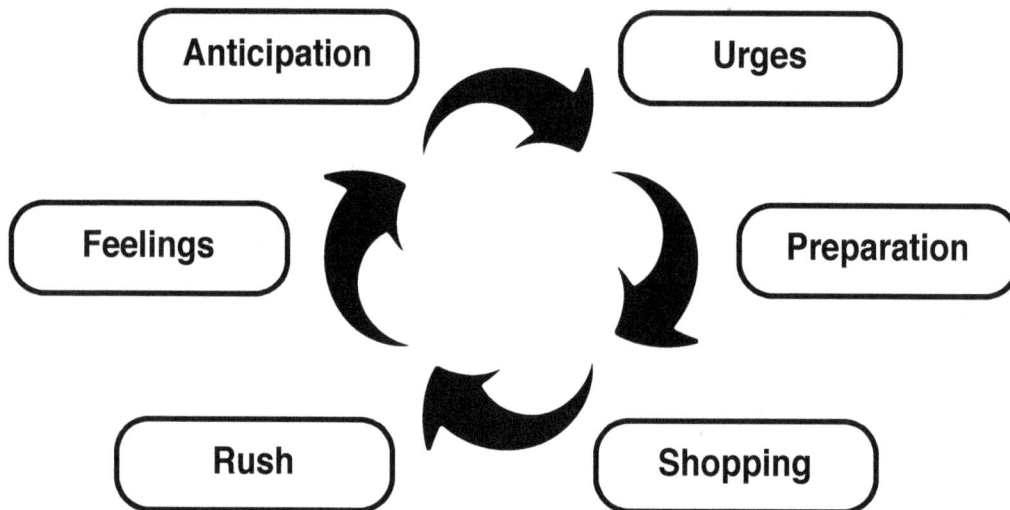

```
        Anticipation              Urges


   Feelings                          Preparation


        Rush                   Shopping
```

Anticipation: Thinking about shopping trips in the future, reminiscing about shopping in the past, or wishing about something special to purchase. This thinking often turns to worry and anxiety and leads to overpowering urges.

Urges: Feeling the urge to shop is usually strongest when connected to anxiety, sadness, anger, or other negative emotions.

Preparation: Preparing to shop by making shopping lists, looking for sales, searching for coupons, compulsively looking online, researching items, and talking to others about upcoming bargains or shopping trips.

Shopping: Shopping in person or online including searching for products, adding items to online shopping carts, physically picking items up in the store, and spending money for items.

Rush: People initially feel a "high" or "rush" from the act of shopping. However, any positive feelings are fleeting.

Feelings: Experiencing feelings such as regret, shame, and embarrassment lead to more feelings of distress and more addictive shopping behavior.

Using This Workbook

The purpose of *The Shopping Addiction Workbook* is to provide helping professionals with cognitive and behavioral assessments, tools, and exercises that can be utilized to treat the root psychological causes of a shopping addiction. It is designed to help people identify and change negative, unhealthy thoughts and behaviors that may have led to a shopping addiction. The activities contained in this workbook can assist participants in identifying the triggers which can lead to an addiction to shopping and teach them ways to overcome and manage those triggers.

The Shopping Addiction Workbook **will help participants to shape their behaviors:**

- Recognize that they are experiencing an addiction problem.
- Reflect and become aware of the behaviors that were part of and arose from the addiction.
- Build self-esteem in positive capabilities outside of shopping.
- Understand the triggers for preoccupation with various aspects of shopping behavior.
- Develop greater self-acceptance and the ability to change ineffective behaviors.
- Understand recurring patterns that indicate a shopping addiction.
- Learn ways to live a new life without obsessing about shopping and spending.

The Shopping Addiction Workbook is a practical tool for teachers, counselors, and helping professionals working with people suffering from a shopping addiction. Depending on the role of the person using this workbook and the specific group's or individual's needs, the modules can be used individually or as part of an integrated curriculum. The facilitator can administer an activity with a group or individual or use multiple assessments in workshop.

Confidentiality When Completing Activity Handouts

Participants will see the words "NAME CODES" on some of the activities in the modules. Instruct participants that when writing or speaking about anyone, they need to **USES NAME CODES** for people to preserve privacy and anonymity. This will allow participants to explore their feelings without hurting others or fearing gossip, harm, or retribution. For example, a friend named Megan, who drives a Volkswagen, might be assigned a **NAME CODE** of DAV for a particular exercise. To protect identities, they do not use people's actual names or initials, only **NAME CODES**.

The Five Modules

This workbook contains five modules of activity-based handouts that will help participants learn more about themselves and their shopping addiction. These modules serve as avenues for self-reflection and group experiences revolving around topics of importance in the participants' lives.

The activities in this workbook are user-friendly and varied to provide a comprehensive way of analyzing, strengthening, and developing characteristics, skills, and attitudes for overcoming an addiction to shopping.

The activities in this workbook are completely reproducible and can be photocopied and/or revised for direct participant use.

Module 1: Emotional Shopping

This module helps participants explore their emotional and impulsive shopping behaviors. It explores why people shop to deal with unsatisfying emotions, ways of stabilizing these emotions, how to control shopping impulses, and how to deal with emotions before shopping, during the shopping experience, and after purchases have been made.

Module 2: My Compulsive Shopping Behavior

This module helps participants explore how people become compulsive shoppers by examining where and when they shop, the various forms of shopping they use, the reasons they shop, the long-term effects of their shopping behavior, and how they can be more mindful to avoid shopping.

Module 3: Consequences of Overshopping

This module helps participants examine the consequences of addicted overshopping in their lives by examining how their shopping behavior affects their relationships, finances, job performances, recreational activities, family life, and personal emotions.

Module 4: Financial Responsibility

This module helps participants be more mindful of their financial responsibility to overcome their shopping addiction by examining how they can identify triggers, avoid temptation, stay away from shopping venues, ask others for help, create a budget, and take responsibility for their shopping behavior.

Module 5: Moving On

This module helps participants discover ways to move on from their addiction to shopping by exploring enhancements to self-esteem, disclosing secrets about their shopping behavior to trusted people or significant others, reframing shopping thoughts, and understanding how shopping is often used to fill voids and meet unmet needs.

Different Types of Activity Handouts Included in This Workbook

A variety of materials are included in this reproducible workbook:

- **Action Plans** that assist participants in meeting the goals and objectives of treatment.

- **Assessments** that allow participants to explore their behavior. Often these assessments can be used as pre-and post-tests to measure the participants' growth.

- **Drawing and Doodling** to unleash the power of the right side of the brain.

- **Educational Pages** that provide insights and tips related to the topic.

- **Group Activities** to encourage collaboration among participants.

- **Journaling Activities** can help participants clarify their thoughts and feelings, thus gaining helpful self-knowledge.

- **Positive Affirmations** allow participants to create formidable affirmations that can be posted and repeated to themselves when impulses begin.

- **Quotation Pages** that allow participants to reflect on many powerful quotes and ways they may apply them to their own life.

- **Tables** that require participants to reflect on their lives in the past, understand themselves in the present, and react more effectively in the future.

References

American Addiction Centers (2019). Behavioral Addictions.
https://americanaddictioncenters.org/behavioral-addictions

American Psychiatric Association (2018). Diagnostic and Statistical Manual of Mental Disorders (DSM–5),
https://www.psychiatry.org/psychiatrists/practice/dsm

Keck PE Jr, McElroy SL, Pope HG Jr, Smith JM, and Strakowski SM (1994). Compulsive buying: A report of 20 cases. *Journal of Clinical Psychiatry.* June,55(6), 242-8.

National Institute of Health (2010). *Introduction to Behavioral Addictions.*
https://www.ncbi.nlm.nih.gov/pmc/articles/PMC3164585

Shulman, T.D. (2008). *Bought out and $pent.* Terrence Shulman.

World Health Organization (2018). International Classification of Diseases (ICD) Information Sheet.
https://www.who.int/classifications/icd/factsheet/en/

Table of Contents

(Continued on page xiii)

Table of Contents

(Continued on page xiv)

Table of Contents

Shopping

Emotional Shopping

Name _____

Date _____

Emotional and Impulsive Shopping Assessment
Introduction and Directions

People who are addicted to shopping follow a distinct pattern in their behavior. They experience negative emotions and then shop in an attempt to rid themselves of the negative feelings those emotions bring on. Everyone experiences some negative emotions, but they need not be a trigger to shop.

Impulsivity is any behavior displayed without thinking before acting or considering the consequences of the behavior.

When shopping behavior happens occasionally, it may not be a problem. However, when one cannot control impulses, shopping and spending will begin to interfere with one's effectiveness at work or school and in relationships with family and friends. It will probably impact one's financial well-being.

The *Emotional and Impulsive Shopping Assessment* will assist in exploring the two aspects of shopping behaviors—emotions and impulses. It contains 30 statements about emotions and impulsivity related to shopping behavior.

Read each of the statements and decide whether it describes you or not. If the statement describes you, circle the number under the TRUE column. If it does not describe you, circle the number under the FALSE column.

In the following example, the circled number under "TRUE" indicates the statement is descriptive of the person completing the inventory:

	TRUE	FALSE
When it comes to shopping and spending ...		
I shop when I am scared	(2)	1

This is not a test. Since there are no right or wrong answers, do not spend too much time thinking about them. Be sure to respond to every statement.

BE HONEST!

If you choose, no one else needs to see the results.

(Turn to the next page and begin.)

Emotional Shopping Assessment

Name _____ Date _____

This will only be accurate if you respond honestly. No one else needs to see this if you choose.

When it comes to shopping and spending ...	TRUE	FALSE
I shop when I am scared	2	1
I feel pleasure when I buy something new	2	1
I get a high from shopping and spending money	2	1
I find that I'm relieved when shopping	2	1
I feel my mood getting better when I have something new	2	1
I believe that shopping stabilizes my emotions	2	1
I shop when I feel bad about myself	2	1
I shop when I am angry at someone	2	1
I shop when I am worried	2	1
I shop when I feel sad	2	1
I find that shopping is an important coping strategy	2	1
I experience euphoric rushes when and after shopping	2	1
I feel guilty and embarrassed after a shopping spree	2	1
I feel empty after shopping	2	1
I am unsatisfied with my purchases when I get home	2	1

Emotions TOTAL = _____

*Go to the next page for scoring assessment results,
profile interpretation, and individual description.*

Impulsive Shopping Assessment

Name _____ Date _____

This will only be accurate if you respond honestly. No one else needs to see this if you choose.

	TRUE	FALSE

When it comes to shopping and spending ...

I will spend money even though I know I shouldn't 2 1

I will shop even though I don't need anything 2 1

I often shop on the spur of the moment 2 1

I see an advertisement and must have the item immediately 2 1

I shop impulsively, which gets me in trouble late 2 1

I often shop and later regret doing so 2 1

I find it very easy to shop online at any hour 2 1

I shop when I feel restless 2 1

I buy things I hardly need at the spur of the moment 2 1

I give in to peer pressure to drop everything and go shopping 2 1

I don't use logic when deciding what to buy 2 1

I cannot resist the urge to shop if someone asks me to join them 2 1

I can't control my shopping habits even though I know better 2 1

I cannot manage my impulses to shop 2 1

Impulsive TOTAL = _____

Go to the next page for scoring assessment results,
profile interpretation, and individual description.

Emotional and Impulsive Shopping Assessment

Descriptions and Profile Interpretations

This assessment was designed to measure your tendency to shop emotionally and impulsively.

For each of the items in the two sections on the previous page, count the scores you circled. Put that total on the line marked TOTAL at the end of each section. Then transfer your total to the space below:

Emotional TOTAL = _____   Impulsive TOTAL = _____

Assessment Profile Interpretation

By circling TRUE, you may be at risk of developing or having a shopping addiction. The more TRUE responses you circled, the greater the risk you have of experiencing a problem with emotional or impulsive shopping.

Emotional and ImpulsiveShopping TOTAL = _____

This assessment measures the impact of your shopping behavior on your life.

Remember, even one TRUE score can suggest you are experiencing issues in your life due to excessive shopping. The HIGHER your score on the *Emotional and Impulsive Shopping Assessment*, the more you need to be concerned about how you shop.

Mark your score on the lines below.

Emotional Total:
   Your tendency to shop and spend money when you are overcome by negative emotions.

_____
15 = Low   **22 = Moderate**   **30 = High**

Impulsive Total:
   Your tendency to shop and spend money impulsively.

_____
15 = Low   **22 = Moderate**   **30 = High**

What was your reaction to your scores? Were you honest? Were you surprised?

_____

_____

_____

Emotional Shopping

Most people engage in some degree of emotional shopping. Buying something new provides a pleasurable feeling, but often for just a short while. There is nothing wrong with occasionally shopping to boost your mood, but you must be aware of how often you do it and whether you feel in control. When you need to shop to feel pleasurable emotions, problems arise.

Below, identify those times when you have shopped to boost your moods.

The Item I Shopped for to Boost My Mood	How Often I Shop for this Item for the Same Reason	Amount of Self-Control I Feel 0 = No Control 10 = Total Control WHY?
Example: *The latest cell phone*	*The first week a new one comes out.*	*0 – I like to have the newest phone to show people. It makes me feel important.*

I've always felt the connection between clothing and confidence,
which is why I probably was such a shopaholic.
~ Jennifer Hyman

Stabilizing Emotions

Shopping and buying can begin to be a problem if it's your main method for stabilizing your emotions. If you feel sad, stressed, worried, anxious, or depressed and immediately go shopping to feel better, you may be addicted or on your way to being addicted. Another clue to a shopping addiction may be buying items you can't afford or if you are maxing out credit cards or borrowing money to support your habit.

Identify your recent unaffordable purchases and explain how you used them to stabilize your moods.

My Recent Purchases	How It Stabilized My Mood	How I Wound Up with Financial Issues
Example: A $500 purse on sale for $275!	I immediately felt better about myself.	I had to max out my credit card, and it will take months to pay it off.

Bad shopping habits die hard.
~ Tori Spelling

What does the above quote mean to you? _____

_____

What are your "bad shopping habits?" _____

_____

Emotional Relief

Many people search for relief from life's pain and problems by shopping. If your emotions feel overwhelming and your response is a shopping trip to make you feel better, what might you do to find relief instead of shopping? Maybe you could talk to a friend, go for a long walk, or play with a pet.

*In the hexagons below, write about ways you could find relief
without shopping or spending money.*

**Forms
of Relief**

Share and exchange your thoughts with others who may have the same issue.

Impulse Control

A need, or an addiction to shop, is tied to an inability to control one's impulses. This often occurs when people cannot resist the urge to shop and spend money, despite the negative consequences of their behavior. The consequences of shopping and spending money typically lead to impaired relationships, problems at home or in the workplace, and compromised personal finances. It is crucial to connect your shopping behaviors with the financial consequences.

Identify your most recent purchases and the financial consequences you experienced based on your purchases.

Purchases I Have Made	Financial Consequences
Example: I traded in my old car, which was in good shape, for a sharp new red convertible.	The old one was not even paid off. Now I have two payments to make.

What did you realize about your purchases and your financial situation?

_____

_____

_____

Feelings Before, During, and After

People who struggle with impulsive shopping tend to experience distinct emotions before they begin shopping, while shopping, and after making their purchases.

Examples:
My feelings before shopping: I was angry at my supervisor.
My feelings during shopping: I don't care about work.
My feelings after shopping: I felt guilty for buying it.

Below, explore your feelings before, during, and after two of your major purchases.

My Purchase: _____

My feelings before shopping:

_____
_____
_____

My feelings during shopping:

_____
_____
_____

My feelings after shopping:

_____
_____
_____

My Purchase: _____

My feelings before shopping:

_____
_____
_____

My feelings during shopping:

_____
_____
_____

My feelings after shopping:

_____
_____
_____

Motivations

An addiction to shopping is much like an addiction to substances. An addiction to substances begins with using a substance and getting an emotional high. The same is true for shopping! You may go shopping because it relieves your negative emotions, makes you forget those emotions, and provides an emotional high.

Below explore your negative emotions and why you are feeling them.

Negative Emotions	When I Experience This Emotion	Why I Experience This Emotion
Anger		
Anxiety		
Boredom		
Frustration		
Jealousy		
Sadness		
Stress		
Other		
Other		

Based on what you wrote, which emotion(s) do you experience most often?

_____

_____

From now on, when I experience _____ (emotion), rather than shopping,

I can reduce my feelings of _____ (emotion), by

_____ (healthy substitute for

shopping). I will promise that I_____.

FYI: Self-Promise is the most important promise ever kept!

A Coping Mechanism

Emotional shopping is often a coping mechanism used in dealing with stress. After identifying the feelings that make you turn to shopping for relief, use some of the following quick relief methods rather than shopping.

Place a check mark in each of the boxes of activities you are willing to try.
Put an X by those you have already tried.

- ☐ Chat with a friend or family members

- ☐ Clean your home

- ☐ Do something creative

- ☐ Drink water

- ☐ Exercise

- ☐ Go outdoors and appreciate the beauty of nature

- ☐ Grab a healthy snack

- ☐ Help someone

- ☐ Listen to relaxing or favorite music

- ☐ Make a non-shopping plan

- ☐ Move around

- ☐ Read

- ☐ Stretch

- ☐ Strike a yoga pose

- ☐ Take a relaxing bath or shower

- ☐ Take a short walk

- ☐ Watch a humorous movie

- ☐ Other

- ☐ Other

Relationship Consequences

Many people addicted to shopping continue to shop excessively even when it negatively impacts their life. As with many other addictions, money problems can seriously harm relationships, yet people with a shopping addiction feel unable to stop or even control their spending.

Explore the relationships that you have damaged, or how another person damaged a relationship with you due to excessive shopping.

Person (NAME CODE)	Relationship	How I Damaged Our Relationship	How the Other Person Damaged Our Relationship
Example: MFJ	Best Friend	I kept borrowing money and promising to pay it back. I never did pay her back, and she got fed up with me.	
Example: BJ	Relative		He liked to buy every new computer that came out. He begged me for money. I gave it to him if he'd promise not to do that anymore. He continued.

Now, for each of the people you described above, explore if and how you can repair your relationships with them.

Person (NAME CODE)	Relationship	If and How I Can Repair Our Relationship	If and How This Person Can Repair Our Relationship
Example: MFJ	Best Friend	I can promise, and keep my promise, to stop spending money and pay back a certain amount per week.	
Example: BJ	Relative		If he shows me that he has not bought anything new for six months, I will consider it.

© 2023 WHOLE PERSON ASSOCIATES, 101 WEST 2ND STREET, SUITE 203, DULUTH MN 55802 • 800-247-6789 • WHOLEPERSON.COM

Self-Esteem

Feelings of low self-esteem can bring on the impulse to shop. The difficulty in controlling the desire to shop comes from a feeling of not "being enough."

In the circles, explore some of the ways you feel "less than" other people.

Example: I am the only person in my friend group not in a romantic relationship. What is wrong with me?

Low Self-Esteem

Afterward, next to each circle, write a strong argument for why that might not be true.

Feeling Lonely

Many people who are addicted to shopping are lonely and isolated. Shopping gives them a way to be in contact with others or gives them something to do.

Do you see a connection between loneliness and isolation and your addiction to shopping? Explore this question by writing about, drawing, or doodling your responses below.

When I am lonely, shopping allows me to…	**When I am lonely, rather than shopping, I can…**
When I feel isolated, shopping helps me to…	**When I feel isolated, rather than shopping, I can…**

Status Shopping

People with a shopping addiction may be more materialistic than other shoppers and try to enhance their status through material objects and approval from others. These people could be friends, family members, neighbors, or co-workers.

What are some of the products you purchase to enhance your status?

A Purchase I Have Made	How It Enhances My Status	Why I Felt Like I Needed It
Example: A very expensive car	*Other people are impressed.*	*Even though it cost more than I could afford I thought it would impress other people and attract them to me.*

What would it take to be less concerned about status or seeking the approval of others?

_____

_____

_____

When we inhabit our own life—stop doing things based on the
approval of others—we offload baggage and trade up to joy!
~ Laurie Buchanan, PhD

Susceptible to Marketing?

People who are addicted to shopping are often susceptible to marketing and advertising. These campaigns are usually designed to exaggerate the positive results and suggest that the purchase will lead to an escape from stress and problems. Advertising and marketing are designed to trigger impulse buying and specifically target the impulsive nature of people, especially those with a shopping addiction.

Identify the various marketing tricks that propel you to impulse shop.

Marketing Advertisements	When I See Or Hear Them	How I Am Affected	How I Can Avoid Them
Direct Mail, Catalogues, Leaflets			
Computer Ads			
Outdoor Billboards and Transit Signs			
Newspaper, Magazine, and Email Advertising			
Pop-Up Ads Online			
Shopping Channels			
Other			

Advertising is the art of convincing people to spend money
they don't have for something they don't need.
~Will Rogers

How does the above quote apply to you? _____

_____

_____

   © 2023 WHOLE PERSON ASSOCIATES, 101 WEST 2ND STREET, SUITE 203, DULUTH MN 55802 • 800-247-6789 • WHOLEPERSON.COM

Retail Therapy and Comfort Buys

People who gain pleasure and escape negative feelings by shopping refer to it as retail therapy. Retail therapy suggests that you can get the same benefit from buying yourself something, comfort buys, as you would from engaging in counseling or therapy. (NOT TRUE!)

What are your comfort buys, and how do they comfort you?

Read the example and then complete the rest of the boxes.

Comfort Buys	How They Comforted Me
Example: Books	• I don't read half of them, but I feel more knowledgeable with them around. • I love to hang out in bookstores with other people. I am less lonely.

Problem Solving

Although there may be circumstances when a new purchase can solve a problem, new purchases usually lead to additional problems. Usually, the things people buy when shopping are unnecessary, and the corresponding financial cost may reduce resources for solving other life problems.

Identify some of your problems and list how you think shopping helps.

My Problems	How Shopping Helps	Does it Really Help? Why or Why Not?
Example: *I don't have many friends.*	*Shopping gets me out with other people.*	*No. As soon as I go home, I feel lonely again.*

List 5 ways you can solve your problems without shopping?

1. _____

2. _____

3. _____

4. _____

5. _____

Impulse Purchases

An impulse purchase habit is a weakness that can quickly turn into an addiction if not checked. No matter how frugal a person tends to be, it is sometimes difficult to resist making an impulse purchase. The person goes to the store and sees something that is a MUST HAVE! The person has a momentary thrill while considering the purchase. The person may even consider all of the positive changes it could make in life. Then, the person buys it and can't wait to get home with the new item and try it out. The problem is that most of the time, the item is not something the person needed or even something the person set out to buy.

What are some things you have recently emotionally and impulsively purchased?

What have you done with those items since you purchased them?

Items Emotionally or Impulsively Purchased	What I've Done with Those Items Since Buying Them

Some Tips for Controlling Your Purchasing Impulses

- **Stop giving in to the Fear of Missing Out (FOMO). FOMO prompts you to be the first to purchase something as soon as it hits the shelves. What do you buy this way?**

_____

- **Don't try to keep up with others. If your friend has the latest technological gadget, it doesn't mean you have to have it. What do you purchase this way?**

_____

- **But it's a great deal syndrome. This syndrome occurs when you are shopping, and something is such a great deal that you cannot pass it up even if you don't need it. What do you purchase this way?**

_____

- **You want to feel better about yourself. What do you purchase to make this happen?**

_____

Needs Vs. Wants

Becoming aware of your impulse-buying tendencies and taking steps to learn how to address the problem will help you make better financial decisions. One way to do this is by being mindful of your budget and your needs versus your wants.

Referring to last month, complete the list of needed or wanted purchases you made.

Purchases I Needed		Purchases I Wanted
_____	⇨	_____
_____		_____
_____	⇨	_____
_____		_____
_____	⇨	_____
_____		_____
_____	⇨	_____
_____		_____
_____	⇨	_____
_____		_____
_____	⇨	_____
_____		_____
_____	⇨	_____
_____		_____
_____	⇨	_____
_____		_____
_____	⇨	_____
_____		_____

Which column has the most purchases? Why?

_____

_____

_____

Ways to reduce Want purchases:
- **Put time between you and the purchase.**
- **Wait a day or so to see if you still want it.**
- **Avoid going to shopping areas if possible.**
- **Find ways to reward yourself without purchasing something.**
- **Stay away from online shopping.**

Quotes about Emotional Shopping

Which of the quotes below speak to you and your current shopping behavior?
On the lines that follow that quote, describe what it means to you and how it applies to your life.

Instead of buying six things, buy one thing that you really like.
Don't keep buying just for the sake of it.
~ Vivienne Westwood

_____

_____

Don't marry a shopaholic if you're not prepared to be a workaholic.
~ Matshona Dhliwayo

_____

_____

The craving for the thing is rarely met by the satisfaction of getting it. And so
we crave more. And the cycle repeats. We are encouraged to want what will
only make us want more. We are, in short, encouraged to be addicts.
~ Matt Haig

_____

_____

The only consolation I had was buying things. If I bought some
pretty thing it cheered me up for a while.
~ Iris Murdoch

_____

_____

What quote especially speaks to you and your shopping addiction? Why?

_____

_____

_____

_____

_____

_____

Shopping

My Compulsive Shopping Behavior

Name _____

Date _____

Compulsive Shopping and Spending Assessment
Introduction and Directions

If your spending feels out of control or causes problems in your life, you might be a compulsive shopper and spender, defined as someone with an excessive preoccupation and poor impulse control with shopping.

The Compulsive Shopping and Spending Assessment contains 20 statements about compulsive shopping and spending behaviors. It can help you gauge if this is becoming a problem area for you.

Read each of the statements and decide if it describes you. If it describes you, circle the number in the TRUE column next to that item. If it does not describe you, circle the number in the NOT TRUE column next to that item.

In the following example, the circled one indicates that the person completing this assessment believes that the statement is true:

	TRUE	NOT TRUE

When it comes to shopping ...

I spend a huge portion of my income on impulsive purchases. . . . . (2) 1

This is not a test. Since there are no right or wrong answers, do not spend too much time thinking about them. Be sure to respond to every statement.

BE HONEST!

If you choose, no one else needs to see the results.

(Turn to the next page and begin.)

Compulsive Shopping and Spending Assessment

Name _____ Date _____

This will only be accurate if you respond honestly. No one else needs to see this if you choose.

	TRUE	**NOT TRUE**
When it comes to shopping ...		
I spend a huge portion of my income on impulsive purchases.	2	1
I hide my purchases from others	2	1
I feel ashamed after I spend money foolishly	2	1
I get excited while shopping.	2	1
I feel agitated if I'm not shopping.	2	1
I feel that the next purchase will improve my life	2	1
I am experiencing relationship problems due to my spending	2	1
I buy many things I do not need	2	1
I have accumulated a large amount of consumer debt	2	1
I continue to spend despite promises to stop	2	1
I am more excited about buying things than owning the items	2	1
I feel a letdown after purchasing something	2	1
I do not use most of the things I purchase	2	1
I spend way more than I can afford.	2	1
I feel a sense of shame after purchasing something	2	1
I have maxed out my credit cards	2	1
I think about shopping a lot of the time.	2	1
I often fantasize about shopping and making purchases	2	1
I purchase things to feel gratified.	2	1
I always buy more than I intend to purchase when shopping	2	1

TOTAL = _____

Go to the next page for scoring assessment results,
profile interpretation, and individual description.

Compulsive Shopping and Spending Assessment

Descriptions and Profile Interpretations

The assessment you just completed is designed to measure your awareness of the impact of your compulsive shopping and spending.

For each of the items on the previous page, count the scores you circled. Put that total on the line marked TOTAL at the end of the section. Then, transfer your total to the space below.

Compulsive Shopping and Spending TOTAL   =   _____

Assessment Profile Interpretation

By circling even ONE YES answer, you are presently at risk of developing or already have an addiction to shopping. The more YES answers you circled, the greater your addiction.

Compulsive Shopping and Spending TOTAL   =   _____

This assessment measures the impact of your shopping behavior on your life.

This assessment measures the impact of excessive shopping on your life.

Even one "YES" score can suggest you are experiencing issues in your life due to compulsive shopping. The HIGHER your score on the Compulsive Shopping and Spending Assessment, the more of an issue you have due to shopping and spending.

Place your score on the line below.

_____

20 = Low   **30 = Moderate**   **40 = High**

What is your reaction to your score?

_____

_____

Were you honest when you completed the assessment?

_____

_____

Who, What, When, Where, Why?

It is important to start becoming more self-aware about your shopping behaviors. By becoming more aware, you can begin to identify triggers and substitute more positive behaviors for shopping and spending.

In the spaces below, explore your compulsive shopping and spending behaviors.

Who is around, and what are you doing? Who can help you overcome your urge to shop?

What has just happened in your life? What day and time is it, and why is this significant?

What are your feelings when you get an urge to shop?

Where are you when you get an urge to shop?

Why do you choose shopping over other things when you get an urge to shop?

Buy what you don't have yet, or what you want, which can be mixed with what you already own. Buy only because something excites you, not just for the simple act of shopping.
~ Karl Lagerfeld

© 2023 WHOLE PERSON ASSOCIATES, 101 WEST 2ND STREET, SUITE 203, DULUTH MN 55802 • 800-247-6789 • WHOLEPERSON.COM

Where I Shop

One of the significant problems with an addiction to shopping is that there are so many different places where and how you can shop. Which stores do you frequent? What do you purchase most in these types of venues?

Write about, draw, or doodle the types of things you tend to purchase most from these venues.

Big Box Superstores	Online Shopping

Television Shopping Channels	Malls/Retail Stores

Reasons People Shop

It is important to explore the various reasons that you feel the need to shop. It is time to reflect on and explore what is occurring WHEN you shop.

For each reason people compulsively shop, explore how you believe shopping helps you, and then explore how shopping hurts you.

Reasons I Shop	How I THINK it Helps Me	How It Really HURTS Me
Example: I am sad	I feel like I can stop thinking about my problems while I am shopping.	When I get home and have bought things I don't need or have the money for, or my partner gets really upset with me, I become even sadder.
I am bored		
I am lonely		
I am sad		
I feel empty		
I feel out of control		
I need some excitement		
I think I am coping with stress		
I try to tolerate negative feelings		
Other		
Other		

Alternative to Compulsive Shopping:
- Talk with a friend.
- Play with a pet.
- Visit a neighbor.
- Walk in the woods.
- Exercise.
- Read a good book.

How Many Have You Tried?
- Make lists before going to the store and buy only what you need.
- Talk to a trusted friend to help you resist the urge.
- Wait a certain number of hours/days before purchase.
- Think about if you need it or just want it.

Forms of Shopping

There are many ways to shop. Shopping options depend on availability, time, access, and many other variables.

What do you tend to purchase in each of these three shopping options?

Technology/Online
In-Person/Malls/Retail Stores
Television/Shopping Channels

Which of the above do you use the most? Why? _____

_____

At which of the above do you spend the most? Why? _____

_____

Which of the above would be best for you NOT to use? Why? _____

_____

Tracking My Emotions

Most people addicted to shopping feel certain emotions when they have an urge to shop. Because of this, it is helpful to track your feelings when you feel the urge to shop. A great way to do this is to keep a journal of those emotions and their connection to your shopping experience.

Use the following spaces to track your emotions for a week.
Reproduce the page for additional weeks.

Days of The Week	Feelings I Experience	My Shopping Experience
Example:	*I get upset and dread going to work. I don't especially like my job or my co-workers.*	*I told myself I would skip eating lunch and go shopping instead. I rationalize that I must work to continue shopping.*
Sunday		
Monday		
Tuesday		
Wednesday		
Thursday		
Friday		
Saturday		

No one needs anything. No one needs a reason to buy —
they buy because they want to.
~ Meir Ezra

Time and Money

It is also helpful to explore your compulsive shopping habits. You can do this by keeping a record of what you buy for one week, how much time you spend, and the total dollar amount of your purchases. Tracking the amount of money you spend for this length of time will help you be aware of the extent of your shopping habit.

For one week, every day, complete this chart.
Reproduce the chart to track time and expenses for additional weeks.

Days of the Week	Where I Shopped	I Purchased	The Time I Started	The Time I Stopped
Sunday				
Monday				
Tuesday				
Wednesday				
Thursday				
Friday				
Saturday				

How am I paying for most of my purchases?

_____

How is this affecting me financially?

_____

Long-Term Effects

Compulsive shoppers often experience many long-term effects from their shopping. Many people find the short-term effects of shopping addiction appear positive (like feeling happier during a shopping trip). They soon discover the long-term effects are overwhelmingly negative.

You must begin to understand these effects to face the realities of an excessive shopping habit.

Which of these long-term effects are you experiencing?

Long-Term Effects	How I Am Experiencing It	What I Need to do to Relieve the Problem
Example: Spending over my budget	*I have maxed out my credit cards and don't know how to pay them off.*	*Cut up my credit cards and, in the future, only buy what I can afford to pay with cash.*
Spending over my budget		
Deep financial issues		
Legal problems		
Problems at work		
Impaired relationships		
Buying everything I want		
Other		

Which of the above long-term-effect issues are you most concerned about resolving?

_____

_____

_____

Who is a trusted person with whom you can talk and who can give you good advice?

_____

© 2023 WHOLE PERSON ASSOCIATES, 101 WEST 2ND STREET, SUITE 203, DULUTH MN 55802 • 800-247-6789 • WHOLEPERSON.COM

Mindfulness of 4 Basic Stages (Page 1)

There are four basic stages in the compulsive buying process.

ANTICIPATION ... PREPARATION ... SHOPPING ... SPENDING

Think about your last "big" shopping spree and respond to the questions in each stage.

My last big shopping spree: _____

_____

1. **Anticipation: You begin to get thoughts and urges to shop.**
   These urges often focus on a specific item or the act of shopping itself.

What thoughts began to pop into your head to prompt the shopping spree?

_____

_____

_____

What urges did you get? How did you experience them?

_____

_____

_____

What was your focus: a specific item or the desire to shop?

_____

_____

_____

2. **Preparation: You start researching and deciding what you want, looking into sales, or**
   debating where the best deals are.

How did you prepare?

_____

_____

_____

What sources did you use for your research?

_____

_____

_____

(Continued on the next page)

Mindfulness of 4 Basic Stages (Page 2)

3. **Shopping:** You actively engage in the shopping behavior. You find you get a thrill or a "high" while shopping.

How many stores did you shop in?

_____

_____

_____

How would you describe the thrill you got from shopping?

_____

_____

_____

What other activities can provide the same "high" that shopping offers?

_____

_____

_____

4. **Spending:** You purchase an item or multiple items. When you are finished shopping, you might be sad that the shopping experience is over and may be disappointed about how much money you have spent.

What item or items did you purchase, and how much did you spend?

_____

_____

_____

What emotions did you have after the shopping experience?_____

_____

_____

How did you feel when you arrived home? _____

_____

_____

What Are Your Primary Reasons for Shopping?

What are your primary reasons for shopping? That can be a difficult question to answer!

Sentence starters allow you to freely write your thoughts without thinking about them. For these sentence starters below, write the first thing that comes to mind!

I shop to ...

I love to shop for ...

I shop on these online stores ...

I shop online because ...

I love to shop in person for ...

I shop in person because ...

When I'm not shopping I feel ...

I wish I could shop ...

I go shopping when I ...

When I am shopping I feel ...

I am having a hard time stopping my compulsive shopping behavior because ...

Online Shopping

Online shopping has made the addiction to shopping more accessible and more prevalent.

Read about some of the reasons people shop online and journal about how each pertains to you:

It is easily accessible with access to technology. _____
_____

It is available 24/7. _____
_____

It is user-friendly. _____
_____

I can shop anonymously. _____
_____

It requires no social interaction. _____
_____

I don't feel ashamed when I'm done. _____
_____

It provides me with instant gratification. _____
_____

There is plenty of variety. _____
_____

It is exciting. _____
_____

I love to click-and-buy. _____
_____

I don't have to leave my home. _____
_____

I constantly receive email reminders and sales pitches from places I've shopped from in the past.
_____
_____

Other:_____
_____
_____

It's Shopping Time!

Think about the time you spend shopping, planning to shop, thinking about shopping, and fretting about not being able to shop. It is often mind-boggling to explore the total amount of time spent visiting certain stores, watching television shopping channels, searching for deals online, and studying catalogs that arrive in the mail. Are there other things you'd rather be doing and accomplishing?

Below, explore how much time you are spending with shopping behaviors, and describe other things you could be doing or accomplishing with that time.

Shopping Format	Time Spent	Other things I Could Do
Example: Online	*1 hour*	*Paying the bills*

Shopping High

The primary emotion that people addicted to shopping experience is referred to as "buyers' high." Compulsive shoppers experience a rush of excitement when they shop, buy, and spend money. This feeling of euphoria is not from owning the purchased item but from the act of buying it. The rush of excitement is often experienced when people see a desirable item and consider buying it. The problem is that this excitement then becomes addictive.

TRY THIS: Whenever you feel the urge to shop, acknowledge the urge, and then do something constructive such as exercise, spend time with a hobby, take a walk, etc.

Below, identify some of these alternatives you can engage in that do not require you to spend money.

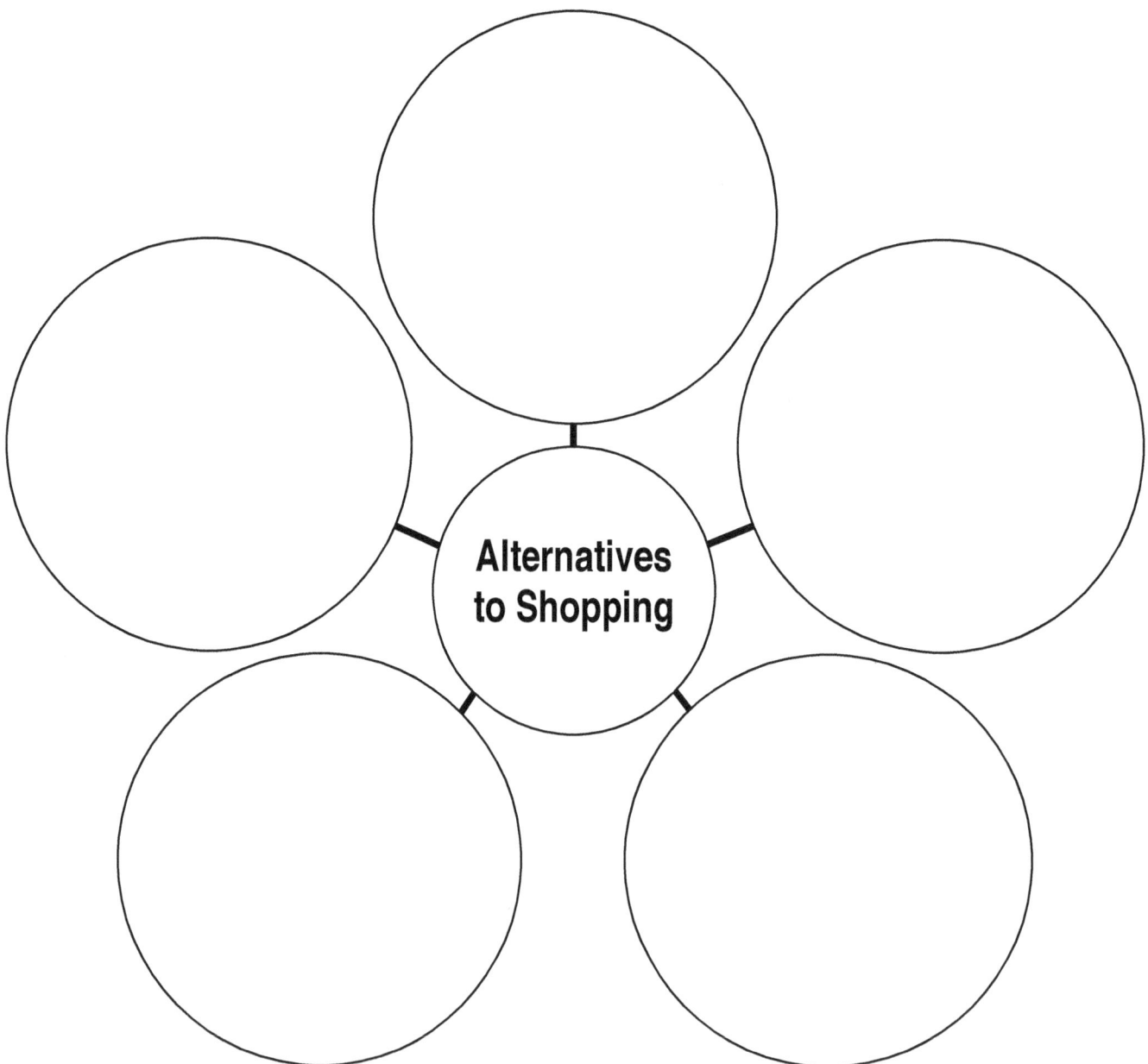

Alternatives to Shopping

Let's Review (Page 1)

Often, people who are addicted to shopping do so because they are simply unaware of their behavior. It is critical to continually reflect and review your shopping behavior to ensure that you are not experiencing an addiction to shopping.

One way to do a review of your shopping behavior is to explore these questions:

■ **ONLINE PURCHASES**

How much time do you spend shopping online? _____

_____

How much time do you spend on bidding sites? _____

_____

How often are you preoccupied with buying the latest releases, gadgets, shoes, purses, etc.?

_____

_____

How much is shopping distracting you from other priorities such as work, spending time with

your family, socializing with neighbors, etc.? _____

_____

■ **PURCHASING BEHAVIORS**

Do you buy excessive amounts of items that you don't need? _____

_____

Do you purchase items and then do not use them? _____

_____

Are you then hoarding goods at home? _____ What types of items? _____

_____

_____

Do you go to extreme lengths to conceal items you purchase? _____

_____

Do you hide your credit card bills? _____

(Continued on the next page)

Let's Review (Page 2)

■ **GIVING GIFTS**

Do you lavish others with overextravagant gifts? _____

Who are the people you buy for? _____

What do you purchase for them? _____

_____

Do you feel the need to reward yourself and others with gifts to mark every single occasion?

_____

_____

■ **OVERSPENDING**

Is your shopping within your means, or is it having a negative impact on your finances? _____

_____

Are you consistently overspending, taking out store credit cards, and juggling credit cards?

_____

Are you running up significant debt which is impacting your levels of stress, your

relationships, and your health? _____

■ **MATERIALISM**

Have you recognized your desire to buy things to keep up with the Joneses? _____

_____

Are you worried about shopping and spending to enhance your social status? _____

_____

■ **OTHER**

What else is important in reducing your desire to shop and spend? _____

_____

_____

_____

_____

_____

_____

_____

_____

_____

_____

Quotes about Compulsive Shopping

*On the lines that follow the four quotes, describe which quote(s)
speak to you and your compulsive shopping habits.*

Caesar of the 21st century: I came! I saw! I bought!
~ Ljupka Cvetanova

Many buy gadgets they don't really need, with money they don't have,
for people they don't actually care for, while infringing their corporeal
and financial capacities, in order to pay doctors and psychiatrists.
~ Erik Pevernagie

Buy, buy, says the sign in the shop window; Why, why, says the junk in the yard.
~ Paul McCartney

Money can buy some things to create happiness, but it can never buy happiness.
~ Ellen J. Barrier

Which quote especially speaks to you about compulsive shopping? Why?

_____

_____

_____

_____

_____

_____

_____

_____

_____

_____

_____

_____

Shopping

Consequences of Overshopping

Name _____

Date _____

Emotional and Impulsive Shopping Assessment
Introduction and Directions

Often, people who compulsively shop feel good in the short-term but experience significant long-term problems. Frequently, the greater the impulse and compulsion to shop, the more difficult it can be to reduce the shopping behavior.

It is vital to explore the problems that your shopping behavior is causing in your life. These problems might include financial issues, damaged relationships, health problems, and problems in the workplace.

This assessment contains 20 statements to help you explore the intensity of the negative effects caused by your shopping behavior. Read each statement and decide whether or not it describes you. If the statement describes you, circle the YES next to that item. If it does not describe you, circle the NO next to that item.

In the following example, the circled YES indicates that the statement describes the person completing this assessment:

Because of my shopping issues ...

I overspend beyond my means . . . . (YES) . . . . NO

This is not a test. Since there are no right or wrong answers, do not spend too much time thinking about them. Be sure to respond to every statement.

BE HONEST!

If you choose, no one else needs to see the results.

(Turn to the next page and begin.)

Shopping Problem Assessment

Name _____ Date _____

This will only be accurate if you respond honestly. No one else needs to see this if you choose.

Because of my shopping issues ...

I overspend beyond my means . . . . .YES. . . . . .NO

I experience constant financial problems. . . . . .YES. . . . . .NO

I max out every one of my credit cards . . . . .YES. . . . . .NO

I go through legal issues due to financial hardships. . . . . .YES. . . . . .NO

I have several strained relationships . . . . .YES. . . . . .NO

I have a low credit score . . . . .YES. . . . . .NO

I am no longer able to be productive at work . . . . .YES. . . . . .NO

I have alienated many friends . . . . .YES. . . . . .NO

I have lost one or more partners . . . . .YES. . . . . .NO

I have a problem keeping a job . . . . .YES. . . . . .NO

I tend to isolate myself when I am not shopping . . . . .YES. . . . . .NO

I am constantly stressed out when it comes to money .YES. . . . . .NO

I suffer from sleep issues. . . . . .YES. . . . . .NO

I believe my shopping is out of control . . . . .YES. . . . . .NO

I undergo emotional anxiety . . . . .YES. . . . . .NO

I no longer want to do anything else but shop . . . . .YES. . . . . .NO

I feel unfulfilled when I'm not shopping . . . . .YES. . . . . .NO

I am not eating well. . . . . .YES. . . . . .NO

I am only truly happy when I am shopping . . . . .YES. . . . . .NO

I hoard stuff that I don't need . . . . .YES. . . . . .NO

Total YES Answers = _____

Go to the next page for scoring assessment results,
profile interpretation, and individual description.

Shopping Problem Assessment

Descriptions and Profile Interpretations

The assessment you just completed is designed to measure problems in your life caused by excessive shopping.

Count the number of YES answers you circled on the Shopping Problem Assessment. Put that total on the line marked TOTAL on the assessment at the bottom of the page. Then, transfer your total to this space below:

Shopping Problem TOTAL   =   _____

Assessment Profile Interpretation

By circling even ONE YES, you are presently experiencing problems in your life due to shopping. The more YES answers you circled, the greater your risk of experiencing many negative issues because of your shopping actions. *The HIGHER your score on the Shopping Problem Assessment, the more of a shopping issue you are experiencing.*

Mark your score on the lines below.

_____
0 = Low   **10 = Moderate**   **20 = High**

Were you honest when completing the assessment? Is your score valid?

_____

_____

What is your reaction to your score?

_____

_____

Do you feel you need to do something about your shopping actions?

_____

_____

Relationship Issues

An addiction to shopping can interfere with one's ability to develop and maintain effective relationships. Many things that make relationships difficult stem from lying about shopping behaviors, shopping so much it causes financial burdens, ignoring important people, work, etc.

In the following spaces, identify some of these relationship issues you are experiencing.

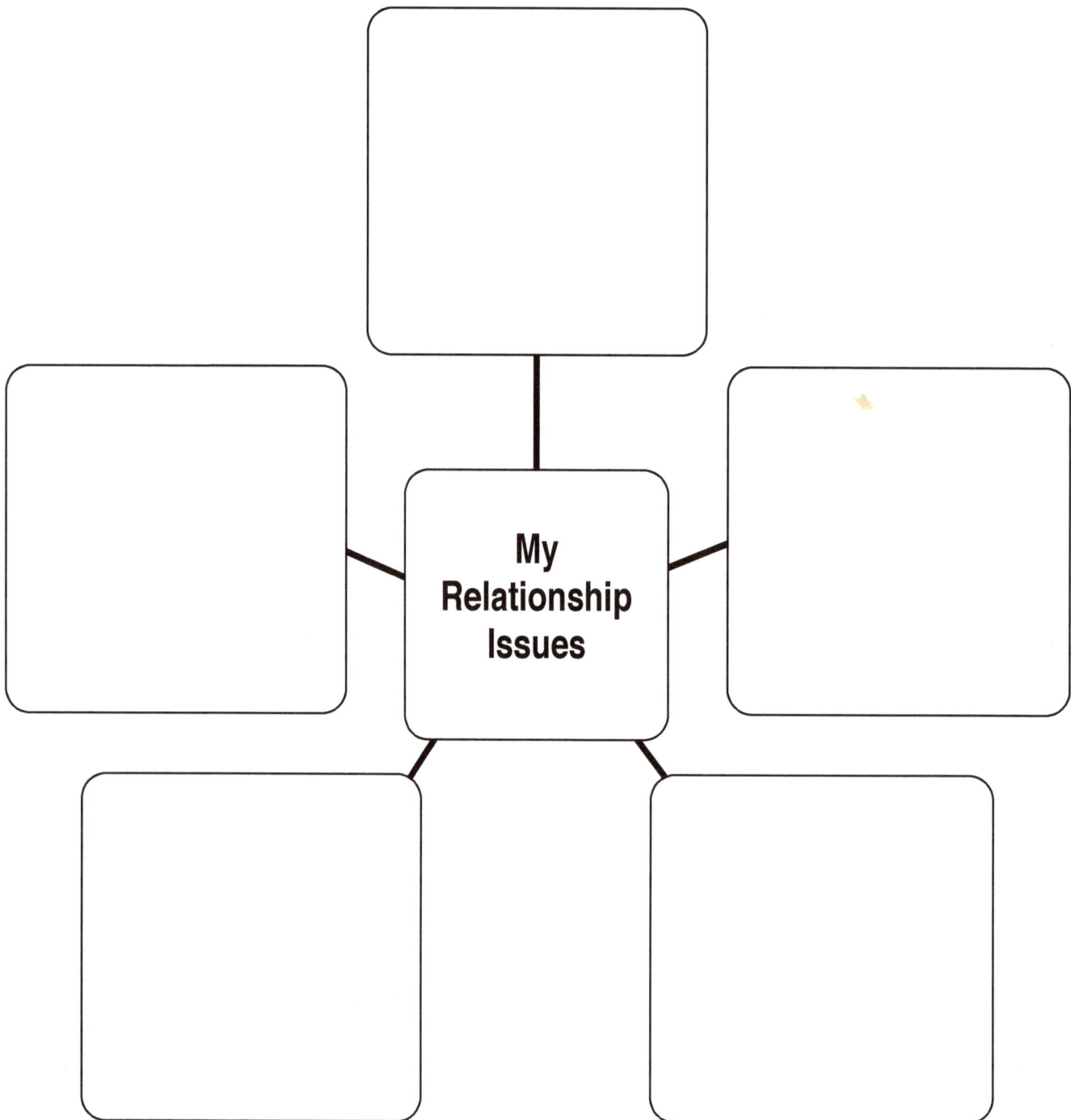

My Relationship Issues

© 2023 WHOLE PERSON ASSOCIATES, 101 WEST 2ND STREET, SUITE 203, DULUTH MN 55802 • 800-247-6789 • WHOLEPERSON.COM

How Are Your Finances?

People addicted to shopping often experience a wide variety of financial problems related to their shopping behavior.

In each of the financial issues below, identify your current situation and provide possible remedies for financial problems you may have.

Financial Problems	My Situation	How I Can Remedy This Situation
Credit Cards	*I have maxed out all but two of my existing credit cards.*	*Cut up the last credit cards and just use cash.*
Credit Cards		
Borrow Money		
Steal		
Credit Score		
Debts		
Bankruptcy		
Electronic Payment Plans		
Other		

Emotional Distress

Emotional Distress: a highly unpleasant emotional reaction

People addicted to shopping usually experience emotional distress. They suffer embarrassment because of their behavior, humiliation, regret, guilt, shame, etc.

What types of emotional distress do you have, and how do you deal with each?

My Emotional Distress	What Occurs in My Life When I Feel this Distress	How I Can Manage Emotional Distress More Effectively
Example: Sadness and depression after my boyfriend broke up with me.	*I took a new credit card and maxed it out on clothes I didn't need.*	*Reframe the event by saying, "Breaking up with Tom will give me a chance to meet new and exciting people. I don't need a boyfriend to be happy."*

Following are some ways to deal with emotional distress:
- Do not blame others for your feelings.
- Let your emotions out in constructive ways.
- Learn from your emotions.
- Lower your expectations about certain situations.
- Own your emotions, and don't let others prompt you to feel certain ways.
- Reframe negative emotions in a positive manner.
- Stop trying to control everything in your life.
- Ask for help from someone you trust about your emotional distress issues.

Problems at Work or Volunteer Job

Compulsive shoppers often experience problems with their job or volunteer work. These problems might be significant, like taking too much time off, or small, like being too tired from shopping and not as productive as the job requires. Other problems might include being late, shopping online while at work, borrowing money from co-workers, and not finishing work projects because of online shopping.

For each day you worked last week, identify any problems you experienced at work due to shopping behaviors.

Days of the Week	Problems I Experienced
Sunday	
Monday	
Tuesday	
Wednesday	
Thursday	
Friday	
Saturday	

I Wish I...

Compulsive shoppers often have many regrets about their actions. Below, write, draw, or doodle some of your regrets about your shopping.

Example: I wish I had more time with my children now that they are more independent.	*Example: I wish I had not spent so much money so I would have more money for my retirement.*
I wish I had ...	**I wish I had not ...**
I wish I had ...	**I wish I had not ...**

Rather than wishing for change, you first must be prepared to change.
~ Catherine Pulsifer

Funding My Addiction

Many people who have an addiction to shopping find themselves searching for ways to fund their compulsive shopping behaviors.

What legal and illegal methods have you considered and engaged in so that you can shop? Be honest – no one needs to see your responses but YOU!

What I Wanted to Own	Legal Methods to Get Money or the Item	Illegal Means to Get Money or the Item
Example: *The latest new IPad*	*I can get a part-time extra job.*	
Example: *The latest new IPad*		*Steal one from someone whose password I know.*

An intelligent person can rationalize anything, a wise person doesn't try.
~ Jen Knox

Neglected Activities

When people are addicted to shopping, they often neglect other aspects of their lives. They may stop engaging in normal recreational, household, or family activities as the preoccupation with shopping takes over.

Identify seven activities in each area you have neglected due to your shopping activities.

Recreational Activities	Household Activities	Family Activities
Example: Walking my dog	Example: Cleaning the house	Example: Helping my children with their homework
1	1	1
2	2	2
3	3	3
4	4	4
5	5	5
6	6	6
7	7	7

Family Conflict

People addicted to shopping and spending often experience relationship problems with significant others and family members. Shopping behaviors frequently lead to martial conflict, critisim, and trust issues.

Below, explore your family conflicts.

Ways I Have Jeopardized Trust and Closeness	Family Members (USE NAME CODES)	How I Can Reconnect
Example: Arguing	*I argue with my partner, who believes I'm spending too much money.*	*Start limiting my shopping behavior and ask my partner for help and support.*
Arguing		
Breaking Promises		
Criticism		
Defensiveness about Shopping		
Hiding Purchased Items		
Hostility		
Isolating Self from Others		
Jealousy		
Making Excuses		
Other		

Which family members are you most in conflict with? (USE NAME CODES) Why?

_____

_____

_____

Legal Problems

People with shopping problems sometimes do something illegal (theft, prostitution, breaking and entering, embezzlement, bad checks, etc.) to pay for their habit.

If you've been involved in a legal issue, explore it below by writing, drawing, or doodling.
Be honest! No one else needs to see this paper.

Now explore some other problems you might have related to your shopping behavior. You might be afraid of losing your property or car, or you may need to declare bankruptcy. Write about, doodle, or draw any potential problems you might have in the future.
Be honest! No one else needs to see this paper.

Stuff I Don't Need

Many people with an addiction to shopping purchase unnecessary or even unwanted items. Some compulsive shoppers have entire rooms or garages filled with toys that their kids will never use, closets filled with pairs of shoes, or overflowing cabinets.

What are some of the purchases you have made but do not use?

Explore these purchases by listing those items in the hexagons below. Next to each purchase, list why you chose to make the purchase, if it was a wise or unwise choice, and how you can avoid purchasing each unwise choice in the future.

Stuff I Don't Need

Personal Losses

When most people think about the problems related to a shopping addiction, they usually think of financial ones. However, various personal losses typically accompany an addiction to shopping and spending, often followed by guilt.

For each of the personal losses below, explore your experience with them and their impact on your life.

Loss of time
Loss of respect
Loss of self-esteem
Loss of pride
Loss of focus
Loss of reputation

Emotional Roller Coaster

People with a shopping addiction describe being very excited when they shop and spend money so that the feeling of euphoria covers up any feelings of sadness, anger, or stress. Once they purchase an item, it's not uncommon for them to feel guilty and attempt to overcome these feelings of guilt by returning purchased items and later going out and buying similar items, hiding them, or forgetting about them.

Explore the emotional roller coaster you experience when on a shopping spree. Describe your feelings in the spaces below.

When Shopping

When Spending

After the Purchase

When You Get Home

Shopping-Related Secrets

There are many ways that addictive shoppers hide their shopping behavior from others or try to act as if a problem doesn't exist. A common sign of a shopping addiction is to hide purchases entirely from partners or friends. The addicted shoppers often lie, steal money, or secretly open new credit cards. They might keep new purchases in the car when they get home and wait until their family members are not around to bring the items into the house.

Explore your shopping-related secrets below.

My Secrets	Who I Keep These Secrets From	How I Keep the Secret
Example: I lie	*My partner*	*I tell her I am going to the movies while she's at work.*

I can't resist buying shoes, bags, and lip gloss. I can never leave
a shopping experience without one of these.
~ Michelle T.

If you were trying to help Michelle T., What would you say to her from your own experiences?

_____

_____

_____

Hoarding Behavior

People who are addicted to shopping often hoard. They do not have enough space to store all of their purchases. They may have rooms filled with collectibles, unused technological gadgets, kitchen utensils, shoes, clothes, books, etc.

Identify the things you hoard, why you hoard them, and where you keep these items.

What I Hoard	Why I Hoard This	Where I Keep These Items
Books I have not read, nor will I ever read.	I like to have bookshelves filled with books. It makes me look smart.	My bookshelves are filled, and I keep buying more bookshelves to put new books on.

Tips for overcoming hoarding:
- Reduce the things you collect.
- Consider selling some of the items.
- Try decluttering for a few minutes each day.
- Donate these items to a worthy charity, library, person, etc.
- Start small, getting rid of a couple of things each day.
- Before purchasing, ask yourself, "Do I really need this item?"
- Think about how often you will use an item before purchasing it.

Am I a Hoarder?

Many people who compulsively shop find they hoard items, their houses become unlivable, and they have spent vast amounts of money on things they don't need.

On the line under each hoarding symptom, place an X on the continuum of how closely the statement describes you. On the dotted line below each one, write why you rated yourself that way. Be HONEST!

I hate to throw things away because I never know when I will need them.

0 (Not Like Me)   5 (Somewhat Like Me)   10 (Much Like Me)

I get nervous thinking about throwing things away.

0 (Not Like Me)   5 (Somewhat Like Me)   10 (Much Like Me)

I believe a particular item will be useful and won't be available when I need it.

0 (Not Like Me)   5 (Somewhat Like Me)   10 (Much Like Me)

I believe that some items will be valuable someday. I collect them and stash them away.

0 (Not Like Me)   5 (Somewhat Like Me)   10 (Much Like Me)

I worry about accidentally throwing away the objects I tend to keep.

0 (Not Like Me)   5 (Somewhat Like Me)   10 (Much Like Me)

I feel embarrassed to have anyone see all my stuff.

0 (Not Like Me)   5 (Somewhat Like Me)   10 (Much Like Me)

MUCH LIKE ME scores indicate that you are prone to hoarding.

SOMEWHAT LIKE ME scores other than a zero can indicate a hoarding problem.

NOT LIKE ME scores suggest that you are not experiencing many signs of a hoarding issue, but you do need to be careful.

Quotes about Overshopping or Hoarding

Choose the quotation below that speaks to you the most and write about it on the lines at the bottom of the page.

We are not cisterns made for hoarding; we are channels made for sharing.
~ Billy Graham

I'm obsessed with shopping. I'll get these urges to buy, like to shop for stuff on the Internet. I search for any kinds of weird gizmos I could get.
~ Tom Felton

On the one hand, shopping is dependable: You can do it alone, if you lose your heart to something that is wrong for you, you can return it; it's instant gratification and yet something you buy may well last for years.
~ Judith Krantz

I don't shop because I need something; I just shop for shopping's sake.
~ Cat Deeley

Which quotation speaks to you? Write about it on the lines below?

_____

_____

_____

_____

_____

_____

_____

_____

_____

_____

_____

_____

Shopping

Financial Responsibility

Name _____

Date _____

The Shopping Addiction Workbook — **FINANCIAL RESPONSIBILITY**

Financial Responsibility Assessment
Introduction and Directions

In our modern world, some major stores are open twenty-four hours a day, seven days a week. Shopping online makes it easier to shop without ever leaving the house. Because of this, many people can more easily become addicted to shopping.

The following assessment contains 15 statements related to three important aspects of financial responsibility for people addicted to shopping. This assessment can help you to gauge how you manage your money.

Read each of the statements and decide whether or not it describes you. If the statement describes you, circle the number in the YES column next to that item. If it does not describe you, circle the number in the NO column next to that item.

In the following example, the circled number under "TRUE" indicates the statement is descriptive of the person completing the inventory:

	YES	NO
When I shop ...		
I use a checklist to stick to what I need	(2)	1
I am mindful of what I need versus what I want	2	1

This is not a test. Since there are no right or wrong answers, do not spend too much time thinking about them. Be sure to respond to every statement.

BE HONEST!

If you choose, no one else needs to see the results.

(Turn to the next page and begin.)

Financial Responsibility Assessment

Name _____ Date _____

This will only be accurate if you respond honestly. No one else needs to see this if you choose.

	YES	NO
When I shop ...		

	YES	NO
I use a checklist to stick to what I need	2	1
I am mindful of what I need versus what I want	2	1
I am aware of my triggers to shop	2	1
I price out large ticket items	2	1
I do not buy something just because it is on sale	2	1

Mindfulness TOTAL = _____

When I shop ...

	YES	NO
I have a budget for the money I have available to spend	2	1
I track the purchases I make	2	1
I am aware of how much money I spend each month	2	1
I have a spending limit when I shop	2	1
I use a budget to keep my finances in check	2	1

Budget TOTAL = _____

When I shop ...

	YES	NO
I leave my credit cards at home	2	1
I spend only the amount of money I intended to spend	2	1
I write my list of items I need at home, then purchase only them	2	1
I bring only the cash I am willing to spend	2	1
I don't take my debit card with me	2	1

Cash TOTAL = _____

*Go to the next page for scoring assessment results,
profile interpretation, and individual description.*

Financial Responsibility Assessment

Scoring Descriptions and Profile Interpretations

The assessment you just completed is designed to measure how fiscally responsible you are when it comes to shopping.

In each of the sections on the previous pages, count the scores you circled. Put that number on the line marked TOTAL at the end of each section. Transfer your total to the space below, and place an X on the line representing your score:

Mindfulness = _____ (Awareness of how much you spend shopping).

_____

5 = Low   **8 = Moderate**   **10 = High**

Budget = _____ (Your budgeting for shopping and spending).

_____

5 = Low   **8 = Moderate**   **10 = High**

Cash = _____ (Your reliance on cash for shopping and spending money versus using credit cards, debit cards, or ePayments).

_____

5 = Low   **8 = Moderate**   **10 = High**

Assessment Profile Interpretation

Even one circled "1" on a scale can suggest that you are not financially responsible when shopping and spending money. The LOWER your score in each area on the Financial Responsibility Assessment, the more significant effect your shopping and spending have on you and your entire life.

Cheat Sheet

A cheat sheet can help you become more mindful and aware while shopping. Think about the last major purchase you made impulsively.

Respond to the questions below to help you determine whether this was an appropriate purchase.

My Purchase: _____

Why was I shopping?

_____

_____

How did I feel?

_____

_____

Did I really need this item?

_____

_____

Was the item I purchased the primary reason for shopping?

_____

_____

What would have happened if I had put this purchase off until later and researched the cost?

_____

_____

What did I do with this item when I got home?

_____

_____

When did I use this item?

_____

_____

How did I use this item?

_____

_____

By taking the time to respond to these questions, you can check in with yourself. This creates some distance between the impulse to buy and the action of buying it. In that distance, you can observe yourself and your motivations.

Avoid Temptation

Temptations to engage in shopping are everywhere!

The best way to refrain from shopping and spending is to avoid situations that tempt you to spend.

Below are some ways to avoid temptation.

Avoid your weaknesses:
- If your weakness is books, stay out of bookstores and avoid shopping online.
- If you overspend at big department stores, stay away from the mall or retail outlets.
- If you get catalogs from where you like to shop, stop them from coming.
- Stop going to the places where you usually spend, especially if you're under emotional stress.

What is your weakness when it comes to shopping?

_____

_____

Say NO to impulsive buying:
- Remember that you do not need to purchase everything that attracts your attention.
- The next time you want that beautiful dress or a new piece of technology, wait till the next day.
- The urge to buy impulsively is a subconscious reaction, we later realize it was a good decision not to buy it.

What are the types of items you buy impulsively?

_____

_____

Plan your monthly expenses in advance:
- An easy way to beat impulse purchases is by planning your monthly expenses in advance. Refer to the budget you prepare earlier.
- Set aside the required amount to pay for your monthly bills and savings.
- Then, with whatever money you have left, you could create a list of things you NEED to purchase.

What do you NEED to purchase after you have paid bills and put money into savings?

_____

_____

Pay less attention to advertisements. Ads are everywhere: online, on television, in newspapers, in movie theaters, in stores, etc. Keep yourself away from manipulative ads by taking these actions:

- Get ad-blocking technology for your computer.
- Unsubscribe from all email and mailings from retail stores.
- Throw away mail advertisements without looking at them.
- Stay away from shopping websites.
- Use the mute button when ads come on television.

Just Stay Away

The increase in shopping venues has made overcoming an addiction to shopping more challenging. One way to reduce shopping is to avoid malls, television, and online shopping sites. People find that they are easily lured by these places and spend a lot of money.

Next time you're bored and feel the urge to go to the mall or shop electronically, try out other activities. Try reading a good book, walking, or visiting a friend or relative.

In each category below, list at least three alternative activities you can engage in.

Athletic Activities
Creative Activities
Family Activities
Hobbies
Physical Activities
Social Activities
Other

Place a star by at least one of the items you listed in each of the sections above and pledge to yourself that you will engage in that activity within a month.

© 2023 WHOLE PERSON ASSOCIATES, 101 WEST 2ND STREET, SUITE 203, DULUTH MN 55802 • 800-247-6789 • WHOLEPERSON.COM

Let Others Help

You may need HEALTHY help and support to overcome an unhealthy shopping habit. If you have the desire (or need) to stop, it would be perfect to allow a trusted friend or family member to do the shopping for you with a list from you or go along with you to shop. This person can help you avoid impulse purchases, stick to the budget, and stay focused.

Identify trusted people you can ask to help you with your shopping and spending habits.

Person I Trust (USE NAME CODES)	Relationship to Me	How This Person Can Help
Example: SKH	Best Friend	I trust him, and I believe that I can tell him about my issues and my financial limitations. He can shop for me when he shops for himself, and I wouldn't need to go to a store. He would help me stick to it.

I'm very lucky to have a strong support system with my friends
and my family. They have kept me grounded.
~ Kelsey Chow

Trigger Points

"Trigger points" are intense and usually negative emotional reactions.

People often feel the need to shop when a certain trigger happens.
Go through the "Trigger Points When I Shop" list and write how and why they are true about you.

Trigger Points I Shop When I'm...	How, When, or Why It is a Trigger Point for Me	How Can I Better Deal with My Triggers Rather than Shop
Example: I shop when I'm angry.	When someone doesn't like my opinion, I become furious, walk away, and calm myself by shopping.	It might help me find a therapist or trusted friend to help me handle my anger issues better.
Angry		
Anxious		
Bored		
Envious		
Excited		
Frazzled		
Frustrated		
Lonely		
Sad		
Scared		
Stressed		

Create a Budget (Part 1)

Many people addicted to shopping may not know how much they spend. It is helpful to use a budget to shop sensibly. Knowing how much you have allocated and what items you need to buy can help keep your spending in check.

Below, list your monthly income AND your basic monthly household expenses. Write notes to yourself (comments or reminders) on the line to the right. If some of the items do not apply to you, write in something that does.

My Monthly Budget

	Amount Earned	Notes
Income Earned Per Month	$_____	_____
MONTHLY EXPENSES	**Amount Earned**	**Notes**
Living Expenses		
Mortgage/Rent	$_____	_____
Utilities	$_____	_____
Telephone	$_____	_____
TV services	$_____	_____
Internet service	$_____	_____
Taxes	$_____	_____
Household repairs/upkeep	$_____	_____
TRANSPORTATION EXPENSES		
Bus/train/taxi fare	$_____	_____
Car payment/rental	$_____	_____
Gasoline	$_____	_____
Parking	$_____	_____
Car repairs	$_____	_____
ENTERTAINMENT EXPENSES		
Sporting events	$_____	_____
Movies	$_____	_____
Eating out	$_____	_____
Vacations	$_____	_____
Other entertainment	$_____	_____
MEDICAL EXPENSES		
Medical expenses	$_____	_____
Dental expenses	$_____	_____
Prescriptions	$_____	_____
INSURANCE		
Life insurance	$_____	_____
Health insurance	$_____	_____
Auto insurance	$_____	_____
Homeowners/Renters insurance	$_____	_____

(Continue on the next page)

Create a Budget (Part 2)

2 TIPS:
1. Track every penny you spend.
2. Any money that is left over goes into a savings account.

Once you start tracking every penny that comes in and goes out monthly, patterns emerge. When you see your spending patterns, you can act on them.

Below, continue to list your basic monthly household expenses. Write notes to yourself (comments or reminders) on the line to the right. If some of the items do not apply to you, write in something that applies to you.

	Amount Earned	Notes
FOOD AND CLOTHING		
Food (total grocery expenses)	$_____	_____
Clothing	$_____	_____
FAMILY EXPENSES		
Childcare	$_____	_____
Toys/games/activities	$_____	_____
Child support payments	$_____	_____
School tuition/supplies	$_____	_____
Pet care	$_____	_____
OTHER DEBT		
Credit card interest	$_____	_____
School costs/loans	$_____	_____
Newspaper/Magazine subscriptions	$_____	_____

Go To The Questions That Follow

What is the difference between your earned income and your monthly expenditures?

_____

_____

How much of that money would you like to save?

_____

_____

How much is left over to spend?

_____

_____

What have you learned about your finances that you didn't know or realize before?

_____

_____

_____

Three Goals

Think about three of your most important goals for doing less shopping. Write them in the appropriate space below.

> *Example:*
> *GOAL: Less Shopping (I will shop less online)*
> *GOAL: Less Spending (I will only purchase what I need)*
> *GOAL: I will save money (I will buy only a new car only when I must)*

MY GOAL #1

_____

_____

Reasons I want to achieve this goal: _____

_____

_____

Ways I will work to achieve this goal: _____

_____

_____

MY GOAL #2

_____

_____

Reasons I want to achieve this goal: _____

_____

_____

Ways I will work to achieve this goal: _____

_____

_____

MY GOAL #3

_____

_____

Reasons I want to achieve this goal: _____

_____

_____

Ways I will work to achieve this goal: _____

_____

_____

Set a SMART Budget

Setting budget goals is essential in reducing your need to shop. Goals will keep you on track, savings oriented, and able to overcome impulses to shop. Once your savings goals are met, you can set new ones to maintain appropriate motivation levels.

Work through the S.M.A.R.T. process below to learn how to set financial goals in your life.
To reduce your need to shop and start saving more money, your goals must be SMART. S.M.A.R.T. is an acronym for:

S **(Specific)** – Clearly define how much you want to save.
M **(Measurable)** – State a tangible amount of savings that can be measured.
A **(Attainable)** – Set savings goals that are achievable yet challenging.
R **(Realistic)** – Savings goals represent a reasonable objective.
T **(Time-Oriented)** – Link goals to a time frame to create a sense of urgency.

Practice being S.M.A.R.T. with one of YOUR goals:

Step 1: Write one of your goals in a few words. (Example: to shop less each month).

My goal is to _____

Step 2: Make your goal detailed and SPECIFIC. (Example: I will shop for books only twice per month.)

Specifically, I will _____

Step 3: Make your goal MEASURABLE. (Example: I will count the times I shop for books.)

I will measure or track my goal by using these numbers or methods _____

I will know I've reached my goal when _____

Step 4: Make your goal ATTAINABLE (Example: I will ask my partner to count my bookstore visits.)

Additional resources/people I need to achieve this goal: _____

_____

Step 5: Make your goal REALISTIC (Example: I do not need to shop for books more than one Friday a month.)

This goal can be achieved by doing the following: _____

_____

_____

Step 6: Make your goal TIME ORIENTED (Example: I will start the first of next month.)

I will reach my main goal by (date) ____/____/_____.

My halfway measurement will be _____ on (date) ____/____/_____.

Additional dates and milestones I will aim for include _____

_____

_____

It's exciting setting goals and moving forward with them.
~ Amber Frey

Meeting Budget Goals

Once you have set financial goals, it is important to begin working to achieve these goals. Below is a process you can use to attain your goals successfully.

STEP 1: Describe one long-term financial goal you have for yourself. It needs to be Specific, Measurable, Attainable, Realistic, and Time-Oriented (SMART).

GOAL:

S = _____

M = _____

A = _____

R = _____

T = _____

STEP 2: Break this long-term goal into mini-goals. This will help you to remain motivated toward your larger goal.

Mini Goal = _____

Mini Goal = _____

Mini Goal = _____

Mini Goal = _____

Mini Goal = _____

STEP 3: List activities that can reduce your urges to shop and spend. What types of activities will move you toward your goal?

_____

_____

_____

STEP 4: Explore the obstacles you might face. Define ways you can combat these obstacles.

_____

_____

_____

STEP 5: Make a detailed action plan. What specific actions do you now need to take?

1. _____

2. _____

3. _____

Stuff I Don't Need (Part 1)

It is time to stop hoarding stuff! You probably spend money on stuff you don't need or even realize you have purchased. Some of these purchases might include television channels you don't watch, subscriptions to magazines you don't read, collectibles you don't care about, and electronic gadgets you don't use. It's time to stop!

Below, list some things you buy that you don't need and describe how you can get rid of them. Think about people less fortunate than you who could use them in homeless shelters and other ways.

Something I do NOT Need	⇨	What I Can/Will Do With It
	⇨	
	⇨	
	⇨	
	⇨	
	⇨	
	⇨	
	⇨	

Stuff I Don't Need (Part 2)
Stop Buying It

Stop buying stuff. Write the items you listed above in the first column. For each one, think about how you can reduce the impulse to purchase the items, and then list some of the various things you can do instead of shopping. (Take a walk, read a book, exercise, meditate, journal, volunteer, etc.)

Reduce the Impulse	⇨	Things I can Do Rather Than Shop
	⇨	
	⇨	
	⇨	
	⇨	
	⇨	
	⇨	
	⇨	
	⇨	

Catalogs

Since you have decided not to purchase anything from a catalog, don't waste time looking through them by hand or online. Addicted shoppers usually receive a mailbox full of catalogs every day and an inbox full of catalogs online. If you are going to break your addiction to shopping and spending, you will need to throw away mail-order catalogs and unsubscribe to online sites.

List some of the catalogs you receive and consider whether you need them or not.

Types of Catalogs I Receive	Why I Want This Catalog	Why I Do Not Want or Need This Catalog
Example: Stuff for the house.	*I like to make interior design changes several times a year.*	*I do not need to buy new furniture. It's better not to get the catalog and not be tempted.*
Example: Book catalog that features my type of work information.	*I find things in there that I can use for my work to keep me up to date.*	*I want to keep getting it, but I can put a dollar amount of how much I am willing to spend a year.*

What types of catalogs do you receive and browse through most often? Why?

_____

_____

_____

 © 2023 WHOLE PERSON ASSOCIATES, 101 WEST 2ND STREET, SUITE 203, DULUTH MN 55802 • 800-247-6789 • WHOLEPERSON.COM

A Concept: Cash... Not Credit

By leaving your credit and debit cards and cash at home, you won't be able to make impulsive purchases, even if you are tempted to do so. If you find something you need or desire, you can write it down and pick it up later when you have the cash to pay for it.

What things do you purchase with credit or ePayment that you can now start paying with cash? In the following spaces, write about them, draw, or doodle them.

AN EXPERIMENT based on, "It is so easy to spend money with a credit card."
For one month: when you go shopping, decide on an affordable amount of cash to spend for the month and keep it with you. Do not charge anything. Write down what you spent or save the receipts. At the end of the month, or when the cash runs out, evaluate your spending—what you spent and what you needed.

What did you learn? _____

_____

_____

_____

Financial Self-Esteem

A shopping compulsion sometimes comes from feelings of low self-esteem. You may feel as if you have to "keep up with the Joneses," look as if you are prosperous, or feel that you have more stuff than other people. You must realize that your sense of self-worth and well-being isn't tied to your personal belongings. Explore your personality characteristics, people, and experiences for which you are grateful.

Take time to reflect and list the non-shopping-related things you are grateful for below.

I am grateful for ...

I am grateful for ...

I am grateful for ...

I am grateful for ...

I am grateful for ...

I am grateful for ...

I am grateful for ...

I am grateful for ...

I am grateful for ...

I am grateful for ...

I am grateful for ...

I am grateful for ...

Be thankful for what you have; you'll end up having more.
If you concentrate on what you don't have, you will never, ever have enough.
~ Oprah Winfrey

You Could Cut up Your Credit Cards!

If you have issues with shopping and spending that are seriously affecting your life, you could (and possibly should) destroy your credit cards. Do not make excuses, and do not jot the account numbers someplace you can access them later. Do not add them to your smartphone wallet. Do not rationalize that you need them to help your credit score. If credit cards prompt your emotional spending, and you cannot control their use, you're better off without them!

In the boxes, write which credit cards need to be cut up!

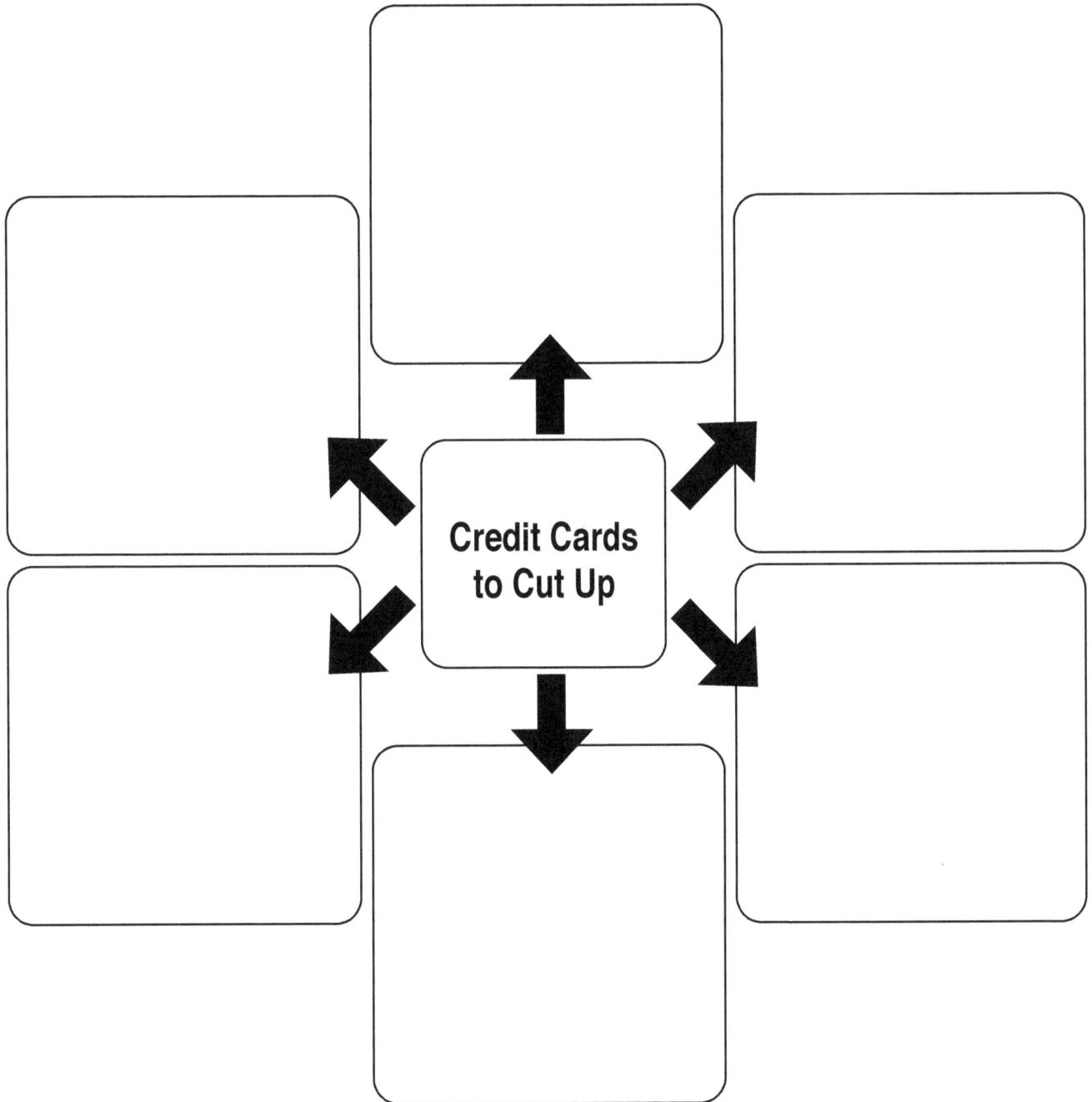

Credit Cards to Cut Up

Quotes about Financial Responsibility

In SECTION A, below the quotes, describe what one of these quotes means to you and how it applies to YOUR life.

In SECTION B, below the quotes, describe which of the quotes "speaks" to you about being more fiscally responsible.

Anything that gets people to think harder about their financial
security and take some responsibility is a good thing.
~ Suze Orman

A cardinal rule in budgeting and saving is to pay yourself first.
Once your paycheck hits your account, wisdom has it that you should
move some amount to savings even before you pay the bills.
~ John Rampton

Adhering to budgeting rules shouldn't trump good decision-making.
~ Emily Oster

I'm very good at setting goals and deadlines for myself,
so I don't really need that from outside.
~ Judy Blume

SECTION A

_____

_____

_____

_____

SECTION B

_____

_____

_____

_____

© 2023 WHOLE PERSON ASSOCIATES, 101 WEST 2ND STREET, SUITE 203, DULUTH MN 55802 • 800-247-6789 • WHOLEPERSON.COM

Shopping

Moving On

Name _____

Date _____

Shopping Addiction Types Assessment
Introduction and Directions

People can be addicted to shopping in many ways. People often experience specific patterns that identify why, when, and how they like to shop.

The following assessment contains 24 statements that assess the reasons that people prefer to engage in shopping behavior. Read each of them and decide whether or not it describes you. If it describes you, circle the number in the YES column next to that item. If not, circle the number in the NO column next to that item.

In the following example, the circled 2 indicates that the person completing this assessment believes that the statement describes them:

	YES	NO
When I shop …		
I am feeling strong emotions	(2)	1
I am escaping stress	2	1

This is not a test. Since there are no right or wrong answers, do not spend too much time thinking about them. Be sure to respond to every statement.

BE HONEST!

If you choose, no one else needs to see the results.

(Turn to the next page and begin.)

Shopping Addiction Types Assessment (Page 1)

Name _____ Date _____

This will only be accurate if you respond honestly. No one else needs to see this if you choose.

	YES	NO

When I shop ...

I am feeling strong emotions 2 1

I am escaping stress 2 1

I am attempting to change my mood 2 1

I am trying to feel better 2 1

Emotions TOTAL = _____

When I shop ...

I seek the perfect item to purchase 2 1

I want to get the best that money can buy 2 1

I research the best items and prices 2 1

I look for unusual items nobody else that I know owns 2 1

Trophy TOTAL = _____

When I shop ...

I go all out 2 1

I figure I can always return what I bought, and I don't .2 1

I shop for luxury items 2 1

I spend way more than I can afford 2 1

Splurge TOTAL = _____

Go to the next page for Shopping Addiction Types Assessment page 2.

Shopping Addiction Types Assessment (Page 2)

Name _____ Date _____

This will only be accurate if you respond honestly. No one else needs to see this if you choose.

	YES	NO

When I shop ...

I search for money-saving deals 2 1

I love bargains 2 1

I like buying things for much less than retail. 2 1

I buy bargains I can't pass up even if I don't need them 2 1

Bargain TOTAL = _____

When I shop ...

I usually lie or hide purchased items when I get home 2 1

I feel guilty when I get the items home, but I keep them anyway 2 1

I often regret buying items 2 1

I return most items to feel less guilty 2 1

Guilt TOTAL = _____

When I shop ...

I love the thrill of the hunt 2 1

I buy things for other people who collect 2 1

I buy a lot of collectibles 2 1

I shop to complete my collection 2 1

Collector TOTAL = _____

Go to the next page for scoring assessment results,
profile interpretation, and individual description.

Shopping Addiction Types Assessment

Descriptions and Profile Interpretations

The assessment you just completed is designed to measure your shopping addiction type.

In each of the sections on the previous page, count the scores you circled. Put that number on the line marked TOTAL at the end of each section. Transfer your totals to the spaces below, and place an X on the line representing your score.

Emotional = _____ **You shop to manage negative emotions.**

4 = Low	**6 = Moderate**	**8 = High**

Trophy = _____ **You shop for unique items.**

4 = Low	**6 = Moderate**	**8 = High**

Splurge = _____ **You shop for luxury items whether you can afford them or not.**

4 = Low	**6 = Moderate**	**8 = High**

Bargain = _____ **You shop for the best sales and deals, even if you don't need the items.**

4 = Low	**6 = Moderate**	**8 = High**

Guilt = _____ **You shop, feel guilty, and then return your purchases.**

4 = Low	**6 = Moderate**	**8 = High**

Collector = _____ **You shop for collectibles.**

4 = Low	**6 = Moderate**	**8 = High**

Assessment Profile Interpretation

Even one circled YES item on a scale can suggest a problem with shopping. The HIGHER your score on the Shopping Addictions Types Assessment, the more inclined you are to that type of shopping addiction.

Self-Esteem

People often overshop because they have low self-esteem and are trying to improve it. They may shop for specific items that will reflect an image of what they believe their life should look like and what they want it to be.

Below, list the items you have purchased and how you thought these items would move you closer to the image of what you think your life should look like.

Items I Have Purchased Because of Low Self-Esteem and Trying to Impress Others	How I Think the Item Will Help to Move Me Closer to What I Believe My Life Should Look Like	How This Purchase Did or Didn't Work Out As I Expected
Example: I buy books I don't even read that I put on my coffee table.	*I think they make me look intelligent and worldly.*	*I try to read the books, and I don't understand or enjoy them, making me feel worse.*
Example: I purchased a very expensive car with high payments for five years.	*I wanted to impress the neighbors.*	*I can't afford the payments, and now the neighbors want me to go to expensive places with them.*

Hints to Help Your Self-Esteem:
- Create positive affirmations such as "I don't need to shop to be a worthwhile person!" can help you. Remember, good affirmations are short and to the point.
- Identify your competencies (cooking, computer repair, fishing, etc.) and develop them further. What are your competencies, and how can you develop them further?
- Eliminate self-criticism in your self-talk. How are you self critical?
- How can you be less critical and turn this criticism into something positive? Reframe your criticism of yourself into something positive.
- What are some of your strongest qualities?
- Focus on what you can change rather than stressing about things out of your control. What things are in your control when it comes to your shopping addiction and what can you do about them?

Why Do You Overshop?

People overshop for a wide variety of reasons. Explore the reasons why YOU overshop.

On the line under each reason for overshopping, place an X on the continuum indicating how much you relate to the statement. On the dashed line below each one, write why you rated yourself that way.

BE HONEST!

I overshop to feel better about myself.

0 (Not Like Me)	5 (Somewhat Like Me)	10 (Much Like Me)

I overshop to avoid dealing with more important things that I don't want to deal with.

0 (Not Like Me)	5 (Somewhat Like Me)	10 (Much Like Me)

I overshop to express anger or seek revenge.

0 (Not Like Me)	5 (Somewhat Like Me)	10 (Much Like Me)

I overshop to project an image of wealth and importance.

0 (Not Like Me)	5 (Somewhat Like Me)	10 (Much Like Me)

I overshop to feel more in control.

0 (Not Like Me)	5 (Somewhat Like Me)	10 (Much Like Me)

I overshop in response to stress, loss, or trauma.

0 (Not Like Me)	5 (Somewhat Like Me)	10 (Much Like Me)

MUCH LIKE ME scores indicate that you shop for reasons other than shopping.

SOMEWHAT LIKE ME scores can be indicative of problem shopping.

NOT LIKE ME scores suggest that you are not experiencing many signs of a shopping problem in those aspects.

Shopping Secrets

Many people addicted to shopping keep secrets about their shopping behavior from others. They keep secrets about going shopping, how much they spend, how many items they purchase, and just as important, how it affects others.

Below, identify some of the secrets you have kept and how you felt after.

Person (USE NAME CODES)	The Secret	How I Felt Afterwards
MDA	On the day of her choir concert, I told her I needed to work late, but I went shopping instead.	I felt terrible. She was the only person in the choir who didn't have a special someone in the audience for support.

Do nothing secretly; for time sees and hears all things and discloses all.
~ Sophocles

How does this quote apply to you? _____

_____

_____

As the quote suggests, how will your shopping secrets eventually be revealed? _____

_____

_____

Alternatives to Shopping

Avoiding a shopping addiction can be difficult because we all need to shop to some extent. Finding alternative ways of enjoying your leisure time is essential to breaking the cycle of using shopping as a way of trying to feel better about yourself. Some alternative ways may include hobbies like collecting coins, outdoor activities like camping, volunteer activities like giving your time to an animal shelter, playing games like chess, social activities like hanging out and having dinner with family or friends, or working crossword puzzles.

In each box below, draw, doodle, or write about an activity you will use as an alternative to shopping.

#1 – An alternative to Shopping	#2 – An alternative to Shopping
#3 – An alternative to Shopping	#4 – An alternative to Shopping

Thoughts About Shopping

It is important to be aware of your thinking about going shopping. People addicted to shopping typically have a stream of thoughts running through their heads before they begin shopping. If you learn to recognize these thoughts, you can frame them differently. When you reframe thoughts, you put a more realistic spin on them. Reframe your thoughts so you can detach from them and not let them prompt you to shop.

Example:

(THOUGHT)

"I am lonely, but if I go out and shop, I will be with other people."

REFRAMED THOUGHT

"I am lonely, but rather than shopping, I will go to the book

club meeting Sherry invited me to."

Below, explore some of the times you compulsively shopped. Then, journal about the thoughts running through your head at that time. Next, reframe those thoughts to something different from shopping.

A Time I Compulsively Shopped	The Thoughts Running Through My Head	How I Could Have Reframed those Thoughts
Example: There was a 2 for 1 sale on dresses at a store I passed downtown.	I have to buy these dresses now, even though my closet is full. I'll be more attractive if I find the right dress.	I have all the dresses I need. I'm attractive as I am. I love myself.

If a problem can't be solved within the frame it was conceived,
the solution lies in reframing the problem.
~ Brian McGreevy

We All Have Needs!

All people have needs, and they want to meet those needs. People who are addicted to shopping tend to meet their needs through the act of shopping! They may not even realize that this is a need. They just do it automatically. It is helpful to be aware of our needs and explore what we can do to meet them. It would help if people with a shopping need could recognize and determine what part of the shopping process provides a reward and meets that need. Then they can learn how to meet those same needs through other means or ask a trusted person to help them figure out other ways to meet them.

Shopping can be an attempt to fill an emotional void such as loneliness, inability to connect with a loved one, lack of control or self-confidence, spiritually void, etc. Some people shop a lot to fill the voids in their lives. When SUD argues with a significant other or expresses frustration over a problem at work, it can spark an urge to go on a shopping spree. SUD shops to fill a void not dealt with more positively, like talking it out.

In the table below, journal about what you need in each area, and how you can meet that need without shopping.

Personal Needs	What I Need	How I Can Meet This Need Without Shopping
Example: Physical	I shop when I need to walk around to reduce the stress that I am experiencing.	I can take lessons in yoga and strike yoga poses when stressed at home.
Physical		
Emotional		
Social		
Spiritual		
Occupational		
Recreational		
Other		
Other		

Voids in Our Lives

Shopping can be an attempt to fill an emotional void such as loneliness, inability to connect with a loved one, lack of control or self-confidence, a spiritual void, etc. Some people shop a lot to fill the voids in their lives. When SUD is triggered by an argument with a significant other, it can spark an urge to go on a shopping spree. SUD shops to fill a void not dealt with more positively, like talking it out.

In the circles, identify the voids in your life that you tend to fill by shopping.

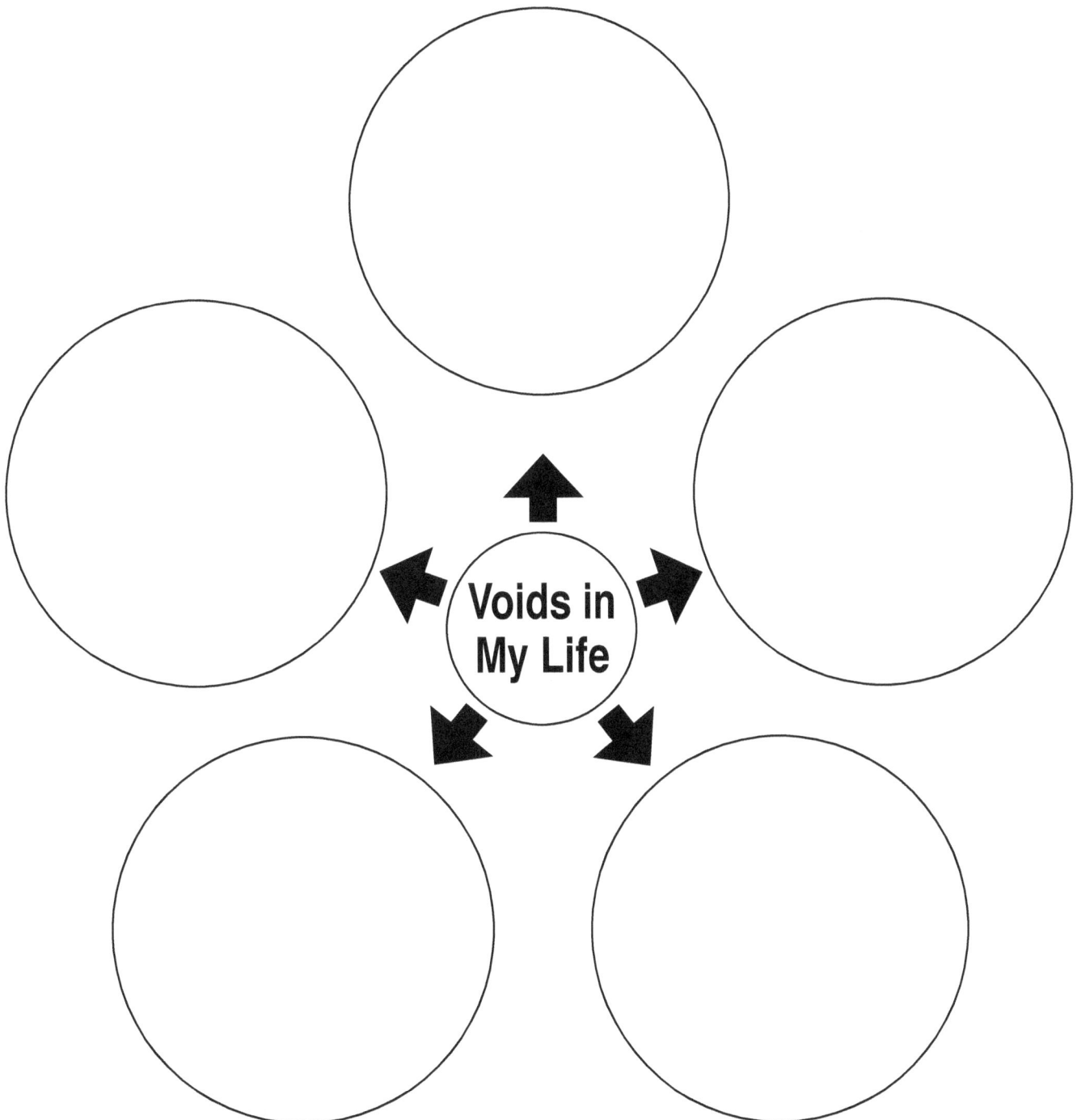

Voids in My Life

Are You a Hider?

People addicted to shopping tend to hide their purchases so that others are unaware of their problem. If you hide shopping bags in a closet or constantly look over your shoulder so that others do not see you shopping online, you could be a HIDER!

My Hidden Purchase	From Whom Did You Hide It? (NAME CODE)	Where Did You Hide It?	Why Did You Hide It?
Example: A formal gown	*MSH*	*At the bottom of the cedar chest in the attic.*	*Because I will never need it, and it was on sale from $400 to $200. I know it's a lot of money, but it was beautiful and fit me.*
1.			
2.			
3.			
4.			

Hiding what you purchased shows that you knew there's something about the purchase that means you shouldn't have bought it. For each of the four purchases above, write how you felt afterward. ***BE HONEST!***

1. _____

2. _____

3. _____

4. _____

Pure Impulse Shopping

If I like it, I'll buy it, pure impulse shopping.
~ Kristin Kreuk

What does the above quote mean to you?

_____

_____

_____

How is the quote like you?

_____

_____

_____

What does impulse buying mean to you?

_____

_____

_____

What do you tend to buy on impulse?

_____

_____

_____

The next time you feel the impulse to purchase something, what can you do to reduce it?

_____

_____

_____

Help Yourself by Helping Others

Rather than shopping, have you ever thought about volunteering to help others in your community? Volunteering is a great way to help others without thinking about shopping or going shopping. Volunteering meets many needs and allows you to engage in meaningful activities, build skills, meet social needs, find purpose in life, and focus on others rather than yourself and shopping.

Identify some of the volunteer activities you are currently doing or might consider.

Type of Volunteer Opportunities	Why It Is of Interest to Me
Animal Rescue Shelters	
Children Services	
Elderly Services	
Spiritual/Religious Missions	
Museums	
Political Campaigns	
Homeless Populations	
Food/Clothing Banks	
Libraries	
Hospitals	
Parks	
Other	

Volunteers are the only human beings on the face of the earth who reflect this nation's compassion, unselfish caring, patience, and just plain loving one another.
~ Erma Bombeck

© 2023 WHOLE PERSON ASSOCIATES, 101 WEST 2ND STREET, SUITE 203, DULUTH MN 55802 • 800-247-6789 • WHOLEPERSON.COM

Mindfulness of the Environment (Page 1)

People addicted to shopping need to become more mindful of the environment where they feel the urge to spend so they can avoid this harmful environment. If you remove the trigger mechanisms, you will also remove the temptations and opportunities to shop and spend.

Below, reflect on the urges you have had to shop and identify the trigger mechanisms.

TIME OF DAY

What is the time of the day when your shopping triggers rear their ugly heads?

_____

How can you remove the temptation?

_____

_____

ENVIRONMENT

Do certain environments make you want to spend, or where you feel obligated to spend just because you're there? These might be certain websites, driving past shopping malls or your favorite store, watching certain television channels, etc.

_____

How can you avoid the temptations?

_____

_____

EMOTIONAL STATES

Specific emotional states can alter your mood and energy, prompting you to shop. When you are upset, stressed, or nervous, you may want to shop to feel better. What other activities (like walking, exercising, lifting weights, yoga, going to a concert, reading an exciting book, etc.) can you engage in rather than shopping in person or online?

_____

What activity can you do to remove the temptation?

_____

_____

(Continued on the next page)

Mindfulness of the Environment (Page 2)

PRESSURE FROM OTHERS

Do you often spend more money than you usually would when you're out with certain people? Who are these people? (Friends, family members, co-workers, neighbors, etc.)

_____

_____

How do they pressure you?

_____

_____

How can you deal with the pressure without giving in and going shopping?

_____

_____

LIFESTYLE

Are you accustomed to living a particular lifestyle that you are reluctant to give up?

_____

How would you describe this lifestyle?

_____

_____

Why is this lifestyle hard to give up or alter?

_____

_____

What about how you were raised has influenced how you choose to live?

_____

_____

How can you maintain your way of life without shopping and spending so much?

_____

_____

Shopping Sentence Starters

Compulsive shoppers have different beliefs about the shopping experience than most other shoppers.

For each of the sentence starters that follow, write about your beliefs.

If I don't buy anything when I'm shopping, I _____

_____

_____

_____

When I see a sale, I _____

_____

_____

_____

I often give in to persuasive salespeople by _____

_____

_____

_____

When I go shopping, I feel like I must purchase something because _____

_____

_____

_____

When I'm shopping, I forget about _____

_____

_____

_____

I will shop even if I don't need anything because I _____

_____

_____

_____

I would rather shop than _____

_____

_____

_____

Time for an Inventory Check

One of the best ways to determine how much you are spending and if you are shopping too much is to do an inventory check. People addicted to shopping often buy things because they have so much stuff they can't see what they already have.

Go through your closets and drawers to identify items you no longer need.

CATEGORIES: clothes, shoes, tools, books, accessories, household products, cosmetics, collectibles, technology equipment, office products, unopened boxes of food, etc.

Below, make an inventory check for as many categories as possible. See items above.

Categories See above for suggestions	I Have Too Much (Yes or No)	What I Have Too Much Of	How I Can Get Rid of What I Don't Need and Stop Buying It

What do you own too much of and continue to spend too much time shopping for?

_____

_____

Where can you donate some of the items you do not need?

_____

_____

Quotes about Moving On

On the lines that follow the four quotes below, describe what they
mean to you and how they apply or do not apply to YOUR life

Everything is created twice, first in the mind and then in reality.
~ Robin Sharma

_____

_____

_____

Most of the things we buy are wants. And we call them needs, but they're wants.
~ Dave Ramsey

_____

_____

_____

We are as sick as our secrets, so I tell everything.
~ Jenifer Lewis

_____

_____

_____

I will go out of my way to avoid the shopping crowds and
the extreme consumerism - I hate all that.
~ Annie Lennox

_____

_____

_____

Which quote speaks to you most loudly about moving on from shopping? Describe how it speaks to you.

_____

_____

_____

_____

WholePerson

Whole Person Associates is the leading publisher of training
resources for professionals who empower people to create and
maintain healthy lifestyles. Our creative resources will help
you work effectively with your clients in the areas
of stress management, wellness promotion,
mental health, and life skills.

Please visit us at our website: **WholePerson.com**.
You can check out our entire line of products, place an order,
request our print catalog, and sign up for our monthly
special notifications.

Whole Person Associates
800-247-6789
Books@WholePerson.com